Jimmy Woods : flying pioneer
LEWIS, Julie
Copy: 1 **Bcode:** 340340046945
Sublocation: N

JIMMY
WOODS
FLYING PIONEER

Jimmy Woods, Woods Airways, 1948-1961.

JIMMY WOODS
FLYING PIONEER

JULIE LEWIS

FREMANTLE ARTS CENTRE PRESS

First published 1989 by
FREMANTLE ARTS CENTRE PRESS
1 Finnerty Street (PO Box 891), Fremantle
Western Australia, 6160.

Consultant Editor Wendy Jenkins.
Designed by Fremantle Arts Centre Press—Jenny Longbon, John
Douglass, Helen Idle, B.R. Coffey, Ian Templeman.
Production Manager Helen Idle.

Typeset in 11/12 pt Baskerville by City Typesetters, Perth, Western
Australia, and printed on 100 gsm Globe Matt by Globe Press,
Brunswick, Victoria.

National Library of Australia
Cataloguing-in-publication data

Lewis, Julie, 1925-
    Jimmy Woods, pioneer aviator.

    ISBN 0 949206 53 9.

    1. Woods, James, 1893-1975. 2. Air pilots — Australia — Biography.
    I. Title.

6 29.13′092′4

For Mollie Woods

ACKNOWLEDGEMENTS

This book is dedicated to Mollie Woods. It is also her tribute to Jimmy. There were times during its writing when I was concerned that she might not be happy with the way I was telling Jimmy's story, but she was unfailingly understanding and generous. I am grateful to her for her support and friendship.

I knew little about aeroplanes or the airline industry when I began this book although I learnt a good deal in the course of my research. I want to thank Frank Colquhoun for his patience and good humour when checking the manuscript for technical errors and for his many pithy observations and recollections.

Much of the source material for the book has come from the Jimmy Woods archive held in the Battye Library of Western Australian History, and I wish to thank the library staff for their forebearance when I needed access to the material without due notice. Additional material was entrusted to me by Mollie Woods. The Civil Aviation Authority (formerly the Department of Civil Aviation) also proved a valuable source of information and I am grateful for permission to read and quote from files.

Many people contributed material, both oral and written, sharing their memories of Jimmy Woods with me. There were former pilots; past and present members of the Civil Aviation Authority; members of the Royal Aero Club and the RAAF Association; there were personal friends of Jimmy and Mollie and many, many people who flew with Jimmy to Rottnest.

I want especially to thank Sir Norman Brearley, with whom I spent several hours on different occasions; and Frank Cocks, who was one of those responsible for the naming of the Jimmy Woods Terminal at Rottnest and who flew Mollie Woods to the island for the official opening ceremony. Mention too must be made of Jean Mackie (Jimmy's sister) and her son William for their assistance in providing the only first-hand information about Jimmy's childhood. I am indebted to Dr Allen Metherell who provided me with his memories of surviving the crash of the Lockheed Electra at Napier Downs in 1942. I am grateful to Paul Rigby for allowing me to reproduce his original cartoons, to Mervyn Prime for making available photographs related to the bombing of Broome in 1942, and to Reg Bagwell for photographs of the Napier Downs salvage operation.

Others who helped me piece together Jimmy's story include Jan Bell, Dr Ken Bellemore, Flora Brodie, Sir Francis Burt, Ned Delower, Ian Driscoll, William Duff, Frank Dunn, Elizabeth Durack, Dame Mary Durack, Peter Griffen, Sir Valston Hancock, Roma Kleinig, Brian Latham, Phil McCulloch, Ross MacPherson, Rene Norman, Bob Pritchard, Rodney Pyke, Leonie Roberts, Jim Schofield, Bill Scott, Dorothy White, Alec Whitham, and Gwyn Williams. If I have inadvertently overlooked someone's contribution it was not through lack of appreciation.

I want also to thank the Fremantle Arts Centre Press who commissioned the work and trusted me to get the manuscript delivered on time; and I am indebted to Wendy Jenkins for her unfailing skill as an editor.

Julie Lewis

CONTENTS

. . . the generous spirit, who, when brought
Among the tasks of real life, hath wrought
Upon the plan that pleased his boyish thought:
Whose high endeavours are an inward light
That makes the path before him always bright;

William Wordsworth *The Happy Warrior*

FOREWORD

'Jimmy Woods? Woodsie? Oh, he was a lovely man.'

Almost everyone I spoke to who had known Jimmy Woods said something like that. Had he never aroused a less favourable reaction? He sounded too good to be true.

The island was 12 miles from the mainland; the ferry could be fun if the weather was good. On windy days it rolled and pitched, and during winter storms anything not fastened down would slide across the decking. Slide...across: slide...back. It took your mind off being seasick. Or of capsising. Of course you could always fly with 'Woodsie'. It was quicker but more expensive, and there was a limit to the amount of luggage you could take. For many Western Australians, a flight to Rottnest with Woods Airways was the first introduction to air travel. Certainly it was mine.

We had to get back from Rottnest quickly. One of the kids was sick. The holiday had turned into a nightmare and all we wanted was to get home. I was scared of planes. It was 1957 and Comets had been falling out of the sky with alarming frequency. People like Yehudi Menuhin were refusing to fly. Statistics didn't count: up there was dangerous.

Somehow Jimmy Woods' little Anson didn't seem half so frightening as a Comet; and Jimmy looked so matter-of-fact and unflappable, with a pipe stuck in the corner of his mouth and wearing clothes that seemed more appropriate for spectator sports than an airline pilot's uniform, that I was sure it had to be safe. I didn't really think about the process of flight. My fear had been emotional; my reason for wanting to fly, practical.

We got to the airstrip and there was the plane. It looked awfully small. Captain Woods sold us our tickets, then he carried our bags to the plane and stowed them. I think we were the only passengers that day; a Tuesday. Jimmy helped us up the steps and told us where to sit. He put my husband John in the co-pilot's seat before strapping himself in, in front of the controls.

'Just give that lever a turn or two, will you lad', he said, after we had taken off.

John turned the lever, not a couple, but a couple of hundred times, or so it seemed, winding the wheels of the aircraft up. I wondered whether to feel giddy, sick or scared.

'Okay', said Jimmy. 'Now wind the other way.'

We were on the way down. How long had it taken? Ten minutes? Fifteen minutes? It was supposed to be the shortest scheduled flight in the world. I'm not sure how long we were airborne, but suddenly the land was again very close and wobbled, first on one side of the plane, then the other. Then it rushed past on either side as the wheels touched down.

It was my first encounter with this living legend — Woodsie.

JIMMY

Lieutenant Woods, RAF, 1918.

GETTING OFF THE GROUND

Live today; the past is unregistered;
The future is unguessed,
The instant is ours.

Mother, 4 September 1919

A thick photograph album, unlabelled, so that faces and places, uniforms and fancy dress, family groups and anonymous people jumble; an autograph album, with farewell messages from family and friends — these are the only personal records of the first 25 years of Jimmy Woods' life.

James Wood (the 's' was added while he was undergoing flying training in 1917) was born in the village of Udny Green near Aberdeen on 14 November 1893, the fourth son of Charles and Elizabeth Wood. His younger sister, Jean, was born six and a half years later.

In 1902 the family moved into the Post Office house at Udny Station where Charles had been appointed senior postman. It was a sturdily built house, of local stone, with bay windows facing the road. There was no electricity, so Jimmy and his brothers, who shared the upstairs bedrooms, would go to bed by candlelight or by the moonlight which filtered in through dormer windows. Beyond the house were seven acres of farmland which the family owned and which supplied most of their needs.

The Woods family home — the Post Office house, Udny Station, Scotland.

Jean's memories, filtered in fragments, give an impression of what life was like at the Post Office house:

> You couldn't knit on Sundays, or sew; you could only tend the livestock. Father was an Elder of the church, but that was later, when he was old. We used to drive to church at Udny Green in the trap. It was the highlight of the week and we would meet people from all around the area. Sometimes the Minister would come to our home for supper and he and father would sit by the fire talking. If he came during the week they might play chess and mother would knit.
>
> We moved to the Post Office house when I was three. I used to watch father and the other two postmen load up their bags and set off. Mostly they rode their bicycles. In winter the snow would bank up and they couldn't push their cycles through the drifts, so they would plod through the snow with the heavy mail bags hanging from their shoulders. It didn't matter what the weather was like, they always delivered the mail. It was the most important thing.
>
> Mother would be busy receiving messages on the telegraph and trying to work out how to manage the new-fangled telephone. When I was older and had left school, I looked after the telephone. She said she never really understood it.

In 1903, when Jimmy was ten, Wilbur and Orville Wright made

the first powered flight in a heavier-than-air machine. At the time this achievement earned little publicity and Jimmy was probably unaware that an event, so crucial to the direction of his later life, had taken place.

After leaving the village school in 1905, Jimmy was enrolled at Robert Gordon's College in Aberdeen and spent the next two years reaching 'a good stage of general education'. A report of his progress praised his regular attendance and highly satisfactory conduct. There is nothing to suggest that he was in any way out of the ordinary. There is no hint of any strong ambitions, or of special talents.

When Jimmy left Gordon's College in June 1907, at the age of 14, he was apprenticed to a firm of motor car dealers in Aberdeen — Claude Hamilton Ltd — and discovered a passion for motor mechanics.

The elder Wood brothers had already become restless, and in 1909 Clarence migrated to Canada, followed a year or so later by William and George. Jimmy completed his apprenticeship and took a job as chauffeur to Mr and Mrs Lawford in Deeside, near Aberdeen. Motor cars were rare and expensive and those who could afford to own them often were unable to drive. It was a job that suited Jimmy well. It gave him the chance to work on an engine as well as drive a vehicle.

In 1909 Louis Bleriot piloted a small 22-horsepower monoplane across the English Channel from Calais to Dover and became famous overnight. He was awarded a prize of 1000 pounds by the London *Daily Mail*.

Jimmy spent several years with the Lawfords. On his days off he would go back to Udny Station where he was made a fuss of — breakfast in bed (oatmeal and bannock cakes) and leisurely afternoons. He would spend the evening either at George Abel's garage or over the road with Dr MacKeggie. Then it would be back to the routine at Deeside.

Letters from Canada tempted him to join his brothers. Instead, after seeing a newspaper advertisement offering the position of chauffeur to a member of the New Zealand Parliament, he decided to go there. His father's cousin owned a property near Dunedin, having migrated some years before, along with many other Scots. Early in 1914 Jimmy was on his way, travelling by steamship, via

Panama.

Before starting work in Auckland (there is some doubt as to whether it was a Member of Parliament or the Mayor of Auckland that he was to drive for), Jimmy visited his uncle, but wasn't very impressed with the rural life.

'I got fed up with listening to the sheep bleating', he wrote in a letter home, 'and couldn't wait to get my hands on the steering wheel of a car'.

In August 1914, not long after his arrival, war was declared between England and Germany. For any man with an interest in machines, the Royal Flying Corps offered great opportunities. Jimmy may have felt that his journey to New Zealand was ill-timed as there appeared to be no facilities there for learning to fly, let alone for combat training.

But New Zealand was not as far behind as he feared. Two brothers, Vivian and Leo Walsh, had made some progress as pioneers of flight in that country. For several years they had worked designing and attempting to build aircraft. On New Year's Day, 1915, the first flying boat designed and built in the southern hemisphere made its maiden flight, piloted by Vivian Walsh. It was the initial step towards the establishment of a flying school in New Zealand.

After the success of their first venture, the brothers approached the Government for help to build planes in which to teach New Zealanders to fly, but neither financial nor material help was forthcoming. Undeterred, the two men went ahead alone, and on 2 October 1915, opened Walsh Brothers' and Dexter's New Zealand Flying School on an old mission property at Kohimarama near Auckland. Dexter, an American, put up most of the money. They had only one training plane — their own home-built flying boat — but soon acquired a second aircraft, a Caudron type-F land plane which they rebuilt and put on floats. By February of the following year, the Imperial and New Zealand governments had jointly approved a flying training scheme and the school was besieged with enquiries from young men eager to learn to fly.

Conditions for entry were rigorous. Upbringing, education and 'social standing' were taken into account. Successful applicants had to pay 125 pounds and were responsible for any extra costs that might arise during training. When the first intake of students

Trainees on Curtiss flying boat, Kohi, New Zealand, 1916. Jimmy top left.

completed the course, they were awarded the required aviator's certificate from the Royal Aero Club of Britain, and left for England and further training with the Royal Flying Corps.

One hundred and twenty-five pounds was a good deal of money in those days and it is unlikely that Jimmy would have managed to save such an amount. While he was not extravagant — his family upbringing would have made sure of that — he mostly spent what he earned; there was rarely anything left over from his wage to be put aside. If he was going to get into the flying school he would have to find someone to put up the money. This was Jimmy's first attempt, and a successful one apparently, to get financial backing for a flying venture. He had a good case — patriotism; if there were other motives he kept them to himself. Possibly he asked only for a loan, certain that in due course he would be able to repay it. It seems fairly certain that his backer was the Mayor of Auckland, James Henry Gunson.

James Wood was admitted for training early in 1917 and for the first time in his life became part of a team. He had always been something of a loner, self-sufficient and independent, but at Kohi, as the students called their training base, he enjoyed the

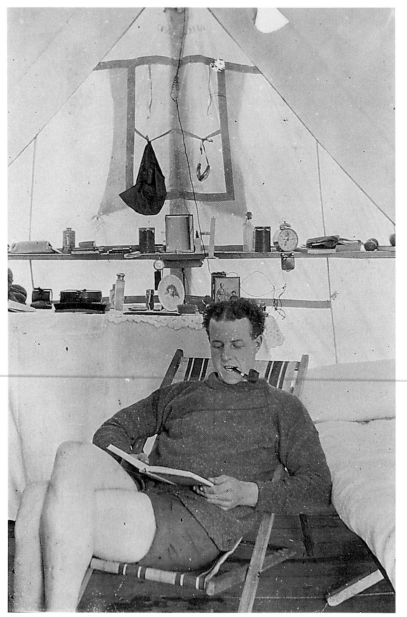

Jimmy in his tent at Kohi.

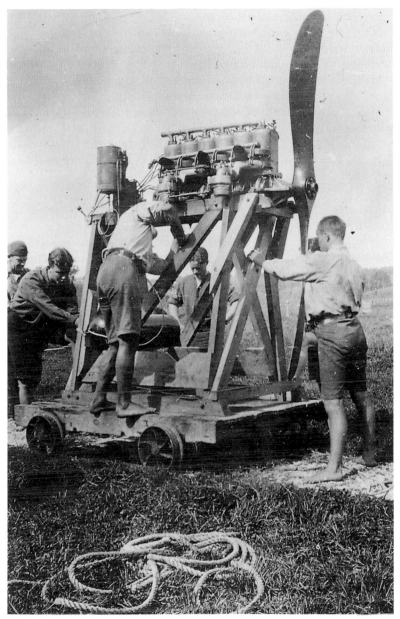

Working on an engine, Kohi.

comradeship of fellow trainees.

The students were housed in tents behind the hangars. The klaxon would sound at 5am in summer and the crews would dress and report alongside their machines which were railed to the water and floated off their supporting cradles. Flying began half an hour later. Their traineeship involved every aspect of flying. They helped repair, maintain, service and rebuild aircraft; they studied aerodynamics, Morse signalling and weather conditions; and they learnt to fly the planes of the time, flimsy structures of struts and fabric. There was no specialised ground staff. The students did the lot.

In the evenings, they would gather in the messroom at the back of the mission house, and on wet nights there was a good deal of jostling to get near the blazing log fire.

During his training Jimmy met Dick Russell and Dick de Lisle; the latter was to remain a friend for several years. Tobacco pipes seemed to be as much a part of their uniform as flying helmets and goggles; most of the photographs of Jimmy at this time show him with his unruly hair subdued by oil into neat centre-parted waves, and a pipe clenched in the corner of his mouth. To his fellow students he was known as 'Woodsie'.

Flying was not without its hazards and students were made aware of the danger of spatial disorientation (though they didn't call it that then). Those early planes had only the most primitive of instruments. There was no artificial horizon and no way of estimating altitude except by visual means. Without an external reference like the natural horizon, pilots could quickly become disorientated and lose control. Some attempt was made to train pilots to cope with the problems of flying 'blind' and Jimmy discovered that he had a natural skill for what became known as 'seat of the pants flying'. The term was based upon physical fact. Pilots learned to respond to the way in which the muscles of the buttocks reacted to changes in height and direction.

Jimmy completed his training in September 1917 and was granted Royal Aero Club Certificate No. 5472 on 29 September. Shortly after, he sailed in the troopship *Arawa* for England and entry into the Royal Flying Corps.

WARTIME INTERRUPTION

There is no honour like possessing a good character.

Father, 1919

The troopship *Arawa* was crowded. Airmen, army personnel and nursing sisters were crammed aboard. They passed the time in much the same way as passengers on holiday cruise ships: playing deck games, guessing the number of nautical miles travelled daily, dressing up for dances and the 'crossing-the-line' ceremony, and strolling around the boat-deck in the moonlight. They took part in boat drill, conscious of the possibility of German submarines and hoped they would not have an encounter with enemy warships. But, being young, war was an adventure, and propaganda had made them eager to do their bit to 'hit back at Jerry'. They were still far removed from the reality and the daily evidence of what war could be like.

For Jimmy, the journey was rather different from the one he had made three years earlier when he had travelled alone and to an unknown country, uncertain of what might lie in store for him there. Now he was able to share the shipboard experience with friends he had made at Kohi. He had changed too. He was more outgoing and although there were times when he might pace the deck alone, mostly he joined in whatever activities were planned. He looked forward to seeing his family again and wondered how

Troops and trainees aboard the Arawa, *1917. Jimmy standing far left.*

he would find them. He had heard that his brother Clarence was on service in France and hoped that there would be an opportunity for them to get together.

The route took Jimmy once again through the Panama Canal. Although he had seen it before, the system of locks through the canal fascinated him. The ship sailed up the east coast of the United States and docked at Newport News in Virginia where Jimmy and Dick de Lisle visited the Curtiss Works. This was partly for sentimental reasons — the plane they had trained on was a Curtiss — but also to catch up with new developments in aircraft design. In the short time that they were there, they were taken up in a land machine, the first time Jimmy had flown in any aircraft other than a flying boat.

George Bolt, one of the instructors at Kohi, received a letter, describing the novelty: '[we were] given tail slided loops and spinning nose dives until we had no stomach left'.

It was a great experience for the two men, an extension of what they had already learnt, as well as the discovery of a whole range of pilots' skills beyond anything they had previously known.

Time telescoped once they reached England, with flashes of

26

home leave interspersed with intensive training. Most of the training took place at a base camp at Eastchurch in the south of England, and the rigours of service life were enlightened by the hospitality offered by local residents. Then the Royal Flying Corps became the Royal Air Force and Jimmy, his training completed, was posted for overseas service.

In February 1918, Jimmy sailed for the Middle East on the troopship *Indarra,* discovering on board another friend from Kohi days, Ross Brodie. The voyage was without incident and the servicemen enjoyed the superficial joviality of shipboard life, while aware of the increased possibility of attack now they were in Mediterranean waters.

When they arrived in Egypt the war was in its final stages. In years to come reports would credit James Woods with having served 'with distinction' in the RAF, but according to the photographs he collected of the time, there was a great deal of tourist activity and not very much combat.

Certainly the Middle East campaign was practically over and most of the flying was of a reconnaissance nature. Jimmy's service records lists nothing out of the ordinary, and the first of his diaries, written in 1919, makes no reference to combat duty. Shepherd's Hotel was the place to dine; the Sultamin Opera House ran plays as well as operas; and there was exciting shopping in Cairo. There are photographs of Jimmy on a donkey, riding a camel with the pyramids in the background, veiled women, the sphinx, tombs, minarets and mosques. There are airmen clowning and riding motorcycles, palm trees, aircraft and ruins.

Early in 1919, airmen stationed in Cairo awaited embarkation orders to return to England. Their war was over, and their days uneventful, but Jimmy did record some day-to-day observations in the final weeks:

> January 2nd 1919. Went up for a flip on the Bristol fighter but the engine went dud and we had to come down, a [Sopwith] Camel and a Neiuport [aircraft] collided on the tarmac, the pilot having a narrow escape, of being chewed up by the prop of the Neiuport.

Finally Jimmy's clearance papers came through, though there

Camp, Egypt. Jimmy centre front.

Jimmy and companions, Egypt, 1919. Jimmy far right.

were further delays before the men could begin the voyage home. A note in Jimmy's diary for 20 January 1919 reads:

> ... after the usual humbugging we managed to get aboard the P&O steamship *Kaisar-I-Hind* and we are absolutely packed like herrings being three thousand five hundred aboard.

There were a few more desultory entries in his diary during the voyage. The weather worsened as they reached Marseilles where they disembarked to cross France by train. It was a slow journey.

> January 30th 1919. Had breakfast then went for a stroll outside as the train stops every mile or so ... In the afternoon we went into Chate de Leur [Chateau du Loire?] and bought some biscuits and just managed to catch the train.

When they finally reached Southampton Jimmy realised that he had almost forgotten how unpleasant the English winter could be, with fog and sleet, and darkness closing in soon after 4pm. He hastened to be fitted with a heavy blue RAF uniform before heading for Scotland and a month's leave. He missed the train and had to wait until the following morning to set off.

From 1 February 1919 when he disembarked at Southampton, until 8 September when he sailed once more for New Zealand, Jimmy alternated between his family home in Scotland and his base camp at Eastchurch, with brief interludes in London. It was a leisurely six months, and boring at times. For days the pages of his diary remained blank or carried a brief note: 'nothing much happening today' or 'the same old thing'. Yet he enjoyed being with his family, with breakfast in bed, outings to Aberdeen, afternoon teas, tiddlywinks by the fire and musical evenings around the piano.

The Post Office house had been named 'Arawa' at his suggestion and it was crowded. Besides Jimmy, there was Clarence (also on leave) and his wife Dolly. Their grandmother was living there too, now elderly and frail. Jimmy and Clarence, when the pampering began to pall, busied themselves doing odd jobs around the house.

Jimmy returned to Eastchurch between his leave periods and passed the time in much the same relaxed way — playing hockey in the bombing hangar, billiards in the messhall, attending concerts in the village or dancing in the Sergeants' Mess with WRAFS from the Station.

The journey from Aberdeen to London took all night but Jimmy thought nothing of the inconvenience for a few brief hours in London. It took an additional two hours to make the connection to Udny, so that of the 40-odd hours between leaving Scotland and returning, at least 26 were spent on the train. Yet Jimmy would undertake this journey as readily and as frequently as in the future people would commute by plane between equally distant places in a mere fraction of the time.

If Jimmy had ever thought of remaining in Scotland permanently, the weather would probably have put him off. He wrote of snow in February, sleet in March and of the rain and wind howling down from the north. Remembering the soft rain at Kohi and the warm summers by the sea, he knew he had to go back. He also realised that if he wanted a flying career he would have more chance in New Zealand. There would be less competition and he had important connections with Walsh Brothers' Flying School. In any event, he had to return in order to be demobilised.

Travelling south from Aberdeen after a particularly cold and miserable few days, Jimmy spent the journey brooding. This was uncharacteristic, but with the compartment to himself he got out his diary and admitted to feeling miserable. Knowing it was not in his nature to be gloomy for long, he added: 'I will soon get over that'. One reason for his depression may have been the ominous reports of Harry Hawker's trans-Atlantic flight which had begun with such publicity. Now, two days after his take-off from New Foundland, nothing had been heard of him:

> May 22nd 1919. Everyone is waiting with anxiety over Hawker's flight. Am afraid he has come by an accident, perhaps got into very rough weather.

Rough weather... A pilot flying across that lonely stretch of water had to rely almost entirely upon visibility to maintain a sense of direction. Once in cloud he would no longer be able to trust his sensory reactions; he could get weird sensations of turning or banking or accelerating or decelerating, even though the aeroplane was more or less straight and level. Jimmy might be able to cope with rough conditions better than many pilots, but he was

Jimmy on leave, 1919.

well aware of the hazards.

Although Jimmy enjoyed the occasional outing with women friends — an evening at the theatre, tea dances and a supper party once in a while — he did not form any strong attachments. Women found him attractive, though, and were pleased to be photographed and to have their addresses recorded in his diary. It seems he kept them all at a distance, preferring the company of fellow servicemen, especially the New Zealanders with whom he had trained.

When Ross Brodie, who had been held up in Cairo, finally arrived in England, he and Jimmy spent a couple of weeks travelling around the Scottish Highlands. Apart from this interlude, Jimmy found the weeks at home increasingly boring. He helped out at George Abel's garage, but as a member of His Majesty's Forces he couldn't take on other employment. There was no indication of when he might expect to be rehabilitated.

To fill in time doing something useful, he suggested connecting 'Arawa' to electricity. This posed some problems because the nearest source of supply was over a mile away and the poles and wires from that point to the house would have to be installed at the family's expense. This did not deter Jimmy. He and Clarence would do all the preparatory work, he said. They cut the poles and laboured all one day digging holes, slapping tar over the base of the poles, levering them into position and making them firm. They finished the job hot, tired and dirty:

> I had an awful job, with the washing of my hands and face, tar having stuck very hard.

At that point Clarence received his sailing papers and went back to Canada leaving Jimmy to complete the job alone.

Jimmy had a surprise in store for his family. On his next journey south he went to Hendon and purchased a second-hand, four-bladed aircraft propeller. He carted it back to Scotland in the train and left it in Glasgow to be converted for the purpose he had in mind. In the meantime an electrician was working on the house. Floorboards were removed and pipes laid. Plaster was chipped to make way for lightswitches, and sockets were prepared for the overhead lights. Jimmy went back to Glasgow and picked up the converted propellor and there was much surprise and some

Propeller light, Arawa, *1919.*

consternation when he returned. His mother and Jean had very mixed feelings about the contraption, though at the time Jimmy was quite unaware of this.

Next day he got to work scraping paint off the metal tips with a blow torch. Then he french-polished the woodwork. When the propellor was fully refurbished he managed to get it up to the ceiling (all 70 pounds of it) and attached it with strong bolts while the family looked on. It dominated the small room, but until the power was connected its full impact could not be appreciated.

They were held up by lack of copper wire. Even though everything was in readiness — the fittings in place, the plaster and paintwork patched, a switch beside each bed and sockets awaiting radiator and electric iron — there was still no power. Days went by. In the midst of all this Jimmy's grandmother died and the electricity was forgotten as funeral arrangements were attended to and the family grieved.

At last, almost two months after the project had begun, the copper wire arrived and the power was connected:

> 28th August 1919 . . . when darkness came we illuminated the house and the four-bladed chandelier in the dining room had a wonderful brilliancy with the six huge lights going.

A few days later Jimmy received his sailing orders. His family was sad at the parting, uncertain of when they would see him again. One of their farewell gifts was an autograph book in which those closest to him made entries. Some were amusing, others more serious. Jimmy was pleased that he had left his family a lasting reminder; one that was both fitting and impressive. Before he said goodbye he photographed the chandelier promising to send a print home after he had developed the negative.

JOY-RIDING

You are a natural pilot.

Norman Brearley, August 1924

The voyage to New Zealand aboard the *Ionic* in September 1919 was one of the most carefree periods of Jimmy's life. Any uncertainty about his career had vanished. A skilful pilot with many hours flying experience, he knew what he wanted to do and had every reason to believe that he would be able to do it. He was free in every sense of the word and the shipboard atmosphere had none of the underlying tension of the voyage Home in 1917.

Bad weather four days out from Plymouth kept most passengers in their bunks. The ship rolled and pitched and fog horns moaned. The dining room was half empty, but Jimmy, who was a good sailor, found some congenial companions among those who still had the stomach for food. As the ship neared the New Foundland coast and headed south, the weather improved and he spent the evenings developing and printing his photographs. The one of the propeller chandelier turned out 'splendidly'.

By the time they reached Newport News, Virginia, their first port of call, the usual shipboard friendships had been established. Jimmy had teamed up with a jovial young woman, Doris Tappin, who was returning to New Zealand to join her recently demo-

35

bilised husband. The fact that she was married no doubt suited Jimmy. He would never have allowed himself to become seriously involved with someone else's wife, so one must assume that, with Scottish caution, he felt there would be no harm in this friendship. An unmarried woman may well have been inclined to regard his intentions as serious. He and Doris, whom he called 'Dorice', found the situation ideal. They enjoyed each other's company, had a lot of fun, and were sufficiently mischievous to encourage the gossips on board who read more into the relationship than there was. In his diary, Jimmy wrote:

> After dinner we got our coats and went for a good walk to show the scandal-mongers that we could go for a walk on the top deck, wet or fine.

When the ship reached Colon, the port at the Caribbean entry to the Panama Canal, everyone looked forward to seeing something of Central America. For some reason getting ashore was not easy. No one seemed to know whether the town was out of bounds to them or not, but Jimmy and Doris and another couple, after giving their names to a soldier on duty, headed for the town.

They had a great evening. They shopped in the markets, trying on huge curved-brim straw hats. They bought bunches of bananas. They went to a cabaret. On the way back to the wharf they were accosted by a patrol and placed under arrest. There was a lively argument, with Jimmy doing most of the talking, which did him no good at all. He was escorted back to the ship under orders not to leave his cabin, even for meals, for the duration of the trip through the Panama Canal. He shouldered a huge bunch of bananas and, to the cheering of fellow passengers, made his way from the deck to his cabin. Jimmy seemed more amused than upset by the outcome of his tangle with authority.

When the *Ionic* berthed at Auckland, Jimmy wrote of parting with Doris:

> ... and we were very sorry to leave each other, being the best of friends all the way.

For the next couple of months Jimmy travelled round New Zealand, visiting former friends, service colleagues and his own relatives. He frequently caught trains with seconds to spare, or missed them altogether, none of which perturbed him in the least. On 16 December 1919, he returned to Wellington; his holiday was over, most of his accumulated pay spent, and he had to find work.

Early in 1920, a New Zealander returning from England brought with him a de Havilland bi-plane in pieces. It was a DH6 with a V8 engine and had a dull blue-grey finish. Not a particularly attractive aircraft, it was referred to as 'the clutching hand'. Somehow Jimmy found out about it and saw the opportunity to get back to flying. Rebuilding the aircraft was a simple matter if he could persuade the owner to let him do it. The plane would be saleable then and if Walsh Brothers could be induced to buy it, Jimmy foresaw a future for himself piloting joy-rides.

How he managed it is not recorded, but on 22 February 1920, Jimmy test-flew the plane at Kohi. He made three flights, each with a passenger, and the aircraft handled well. As a result, Walsh Brothers bought it for 400 pounds and Jimmy was retained to give exhibitions and joy-rides in Hamilton. These first demonstrations were followed by others at Napier, Palmerston, Wellington, Whangarie and New Plymouth. Aeronautics was still a novelty and the thrill of being up there in a tiny plane defying gravity appealed to the adventurous. Former airmen had a certain glamour too, and Jimmy received a good deal of publicity.

Sometime in April, the Walshes signed a contract with Gisborne's Waikanae Beach Improvement Society to participate in a three-day fund-raising carnival. This was to include flights 'piloted by Jim Woods, late RAF . . . from the Gisborne Park Race Course', and the first aeroplane flight in Gisborne would be auctioned. 'Do not miss on any account the most fascinating and exhilarating sport of the age', urged the *Poverty Bay Herald*.

The DH6 was dismantled in Auckland and packed into half-a-dozen cases for the journey to Gisborne. It took Jimmy three days to put it together again. Then, after giving it a test flight, he was ready for his lucky passengers. Ten flights were planned, the first three to be sold by auction, the rest by ordinary booking. Bidding for the privilege of being the first passenger ever to fly in Gisborne was spirited and reached 31 pounds.

A Mr Fisken was the successful bidder. At the appointed time he climbed into the passenger seat. Jimmy sat at the controls and one

37

Joy-riding, New Zealand, 1920. Jimmy with the DH6 — 'the clutching hand'.

of the Walsh Brothers' men stood by the propeller. Jimmy switched on and cried 'contact', hoping the magneto would fire first time. With the prop turning, the engine running and his finger controlling the blip switch on the joystick (those planes would not idle), he was almost ready to begin his run to take-off. The plane had no brakes, except for a tail skid — a bit of wood that dragged along in the dirt — so two chocks had been placed in front of the wheels to prevent the machine moving. With 'chocks away!' Jimmy began to taxi, the blip, blip, blip controlling his speed. He taxied to the downwind boundary of the course to get the longest run to take-off into the wind. Fisken sat there. The preliminaries seemed to take forever.

The little DH6, at full throttle now, tore across the racecourse and lifted off. There was a cheer from the crowd as she rose — circling the course and banking as she climbed to 2000 feet — and made off towards the city. Returning, she circled several times before gradually losing height and landing at the starting point into the wind.

The second flight was equally successful.

After the third passenger, Otto Hansen, was safely strapped in, the plane took off again. She climbed to about 200 feet when, according to a newspaper report, a petrol pipe burst and the engine stalled. Jimmy managed to land the plane and neither he nor Hansen was injured although the undercarriage of the aircraft had been damaged. All further flights were cancelled.

George Bolt, one of Walsh Brothers' senior instructors, was quite critical and seemed to doubt the burst fuel-line story, suggesting that Jimmy had simply let the aircraft stall. This, of course, was something that could easily happen, often with a far more serious result than on this occasion. Jimmy's services, however, were dispensed with. When the plane was again airworthy George Bolt took over as pilot and Otto Hansen was able to complete his interrupted flight.

Jimmy had visited Dick de Lisle in November of the previous year, and during this time together the men had talked about plans for the future. Dick, like Jimmy, was anxious to continue his career as an aviator. Discussion turned to the possibility of setting up a flying business in partnership, but they had not gone beyond the talking stage, tossing ideas around and considering alternatives with young men's impatience and idealism. They had very little money, so, they reasoned, unless they could find backers it was unlikely that any of their schemes would come to anything. Even second-hand planes were expensive and could only be bought in England where war surplus aircraft were on sale. In any case, Walsh Brothers had a monopoly on all commercial flying ventures. They were well established, had access to aircraft and pilots and also a source of income from their flying school and flying demonstrations. Nevertheless, Woods and de Lisle found the Walshes a bit lacking in business acumen and felt that some dynamic opposition might pay off. There was always the possibility too, that the Government would step in and provide a service that so far had only been offered privately. When the two men parted, nothing had been resolved, but a great deal had been considered.

When Jimmy found himself out of a job after the incident at Gisborne, he got in touch with de Lisle again. It seemed to him that if he was to go to England he might be able to purchase a couple of second-hand planes, ship them out, and he and de Lisle could set up a company offering joy-rides and demonstrations of aerobatics. De Lisle was certainly interested and Jimmy wasted no time applying for a passport. A little more than a month after the DH6 crash, he was on his way to England once more. Soon after his arrival he received a long letter from de Lisle:

4 July 1920

Dear Jim,

... Walsh is fixing up the old bus [the DH6] and she will be flying some time this week. They have lost some great flying days since the crash. At last the Government are doing something in regard to Kohi.

... I understand it is wanted as a refresher station for service pilots and also as a service station for mails etc. If this is so it is bad for us and we must watch ourseyes. It amounts to this, Jim, if the Government are starting a postal and passenger service as well we cannot compete with them.

For that matter we could not compete with Walshs' if they woke up a bit to biz. so we are reduced to relying on joy rides to keep us going. I am beginning to think it would be better to bring out only one bus with plenty of spares. It would mean less initial expense and so, should our reckoning be out, less total loss.

we can get a lot of flying out of one bus and if things go on an average 50% as well as your Hamilton trip we should clear a few hundred each . . . it would be easy to get a larger backing on the strength of our books.

Just quietly I don't like the Government taking over Kohi as I think it will block us for long distance trips.

Jimmy made enquiries about the purchase of an aircraft from the Aircraft Disposal Company and the response was encouraging. News from New Zealand was not. As a result of successful experimental flights made by George Bolt between Auckland and Whangarie in March and April, the Postal Department awarded a contract to Walsh Brothers and Dexter Ltd to operate an aerial mail service over that route for six days a week during the winter of 1921. That avenue then, as far as Woods and de Lisle were concerned, was closed. Then Jimmy learnt that Dick Russell, another good friend from training days at Kohi, who had joined

40

Walsh Brothers as a demonstration pilot, had been killed in one of New Zealand's worst aviation disasters to that date. Two passengers had also died in the crash.

These factors alone may not have deterred Jimmy from returning to New Zealand, but something quite unexpected turned up which changed the course of his life.

William Hadden owned a farm at Gallaton near Stonehaven just south of Aberdeen. He was a friend of the Wood family and had followed Jimmy's career with interest. Recently he had bought a small plane — an Avro 504K bi-plane — which was still in England and he wanted it flown back to his farm. Jimmy had obtained a commercial pilot's licence so when he saw Hadden's advertisement in an Aberdeen newspaper, he contacted him. Not surprisingly, he got the job. A newspaper ran the headline:

STONEHAVEN FARMER TRAVELS TO MARKET IN ABERDEEN
BY AEROPLANE

It was a familiar story after that. Hadden could see that the novelty of joy-rides and demonstration flying had enormous appeal, especially when the pilot was a local man who had already earned himself something of a reputation as a flyer. He employed Jimmy to pilot pleasure flights in and around Aberdeen, charging between 5 shillings and 12 shillings and sixpence depending on the length of flight and the distance covered. Curious bystanders would crowd around the plane and there were times when special guards had to be employed to control them. Jean Wood kept the souvenir card of her flight from Stonehaven in 1921, but there is no record of Jim's parents ever having gone up.

The flights went on throughout 1921 and well into 1922. During one flight, when Jimmy asked his passenger whether he was enjoying himself, according to Jean the man replied, 'Ca awa Laddie yer dien fine. Awl nivver get nearer heaven.'

Inevitably there came the time when interest waned. The market had reached saturation point. Jimmy had to think of something else.

In 1923 he had the idea of offering a passenger service to the Orkney and Shetland islands to the far north of Scotland. These islands were accessible only by sea; the passage was rough and at times, especially in winter, impossible. To offer an air service for

Ready for take-off, Scotland, 1921.

passengers seemed to be a way of keeping the lines of communication open and also a useful business for himself. Jimmy wrote to the Air Ministry about the idea, hoping to be able to attract a subsidy. However when Imperial Air Transport had been formed, the Air Council had agreed not to grant subsidies to any other commercial air transport.

If the Air Ministry couldn't subsidise his service, Jimmy decided to include carriage of mails between Aberdeen and the islands and wrote to the Post Master at Aberdeen about the matter. As might be expected, the exchange of correspondence took a long time and negotiations never really got going. Then, as had happened twice before, Jimmy saw an advertisement in the newspaper which would open up a new career in another country.

Norman Brearley was a Western Australian then in England recruiting pilots for his small airline, Western Australian Airways, which operated a mail service from Perth, Western Australia, and the ports on its north west coast. A pilots' strike had reduced his crew to only two pilots and his brother Stan. In addition to recruiting pilots, Brearley was in England to acquire the de Havilland agency for Western Australia on behalf of Western Australian Airways.

The idea of going to Australia appealed to Jimmy. Weather conditions there were reported to be very good for flying. The airline industry was in its infancy and the way was open for all sorts of opportunities. Jimmy rarely day-dreamed, but he could imagine a future which offered possibilities that would never come his way in Britain and he responded immediately.

The first meeting between Major Norman Brearley and Lieutenant James Woods was fairly formal and took place at the Australian Agent General's Office in the Strand. Jimmy explained that he would like to be considered as a contract flying staff member. Brearley, cautiously, advised that his pilots had to have above average ability.

At that initial meeting Brearley explained the requirements and conditions of service with WA Airways and suggested that Jimmy think it over for a few days.

It didn't take Jimmy long to make up his mind. He wrote to Brearley almost immediately and a few days later received a short note in reply suggesting a further meeting. On this occasion Brearley told Jimmy that if he were to find his own way to Australia...

'I am going there', said Jimmy. 'I intend to go.'

'Well', said Brearley, 'when you get there I'll test you. My tests are very exacting.' He thought for a moment, then added, 'or I can borrow an aeroplane from de Havillands and test you in that.'

'That might save a bit of time', said Jimmy, 'if you make a decision here'.

Arrangements were made to borrow an aeroplane from de Havillands at Staglane Aerodrome in London and Jimmy was given a test flight. Major Brearley was impressed with his skill.

'You are a natural pilot', he said. 'All you want from me now is the full polishing up in your flying technique. Your standard will be pushed up if you come to Western Australia.'

Less than a month later Jimmy was ready to leave.

PILOT WOODS

Jimmy with de Havilland 50 bi-plane, Western Australian Airways, 1926.

CONTRACT FLYER

The other lads didn't have a chance with me. They'd say, "Oh, I know. Jimmy's got you!"

Mollie

Jimmy managed to miss his connection due to a train delay and the RMS *Ormonde* sailed for Australia without him. Unperturbed, he arranged to catch a train to Folkestone five days later, crossed the Channel and eventually boarded the *Ormonde* at Toulon. Shipboard life was familiar and held few surprises, though this time the English cricket team was on board, en route for the Test series in Australia, and Jimmy struck up a casual friendship with several members.

He arrived at Fremantle on 14 October 1924 and put up at the Metropole Hotel in Perth.

The weather was a surprise. Where were the blue skies and the hot sun he had been told about? On the way to Perth he was struck by the scruffiness of some of the buildings. There was a lot of corrugated iron roofing, unpainted weatherboard, and the street verges were ragged with long grass. For someone of Woods' orderly nature, the untidiness was something of a shock.

A week after his arrival — a week spent watching the Test cricketers — Jimmy was given his first assignment; to fly the DH50 to Geraldton and Carnarvon, and he recorded a few brief details in his diary:

> 23rd October 1924. Rose at 4am. Proceeded to aerodrome, 15 miles out, and left aerodrome at 6.15. Landed at Geraldton to drop mail and arrived Carnarvon 3.55pm. Weather rather bumpy in latter stage. A few kangaroos to be seen. The country very rough.
> 24th. Rose at 5am . . . took to the air at 6.10. Landed at Onslow and Roebourne on Whim Creek to leave mails etc. and arrived Port Hedland 3.30. Very hot winds blowing Roebourne and sand storms looming around 3,000 feet. Very bumpy flying near Whim Creek.

Those early aircraft had none of the comfort of later planes; and very few instruments. Flying them meant being deafened by the noise of the engines and affected by variations in air pressure. Passengers and crew in the open cockpit would be buffeted by wind, drenched by rain and blistered by sun. The men who flew the planes loved them, but even they could be affected by bumpy conditions. For passengers the experience may have been exhilarating, but it could also be unpleasant and frightening.

Jimmy spent a few days during that first assignment at Port Hedland, enjoying his first glimpse of the North West.

> 26th. . . . Had morning tea at Lake Restore and a stroll in the afternoon and fishing later on. Caught nothing. The fish caught everything.
> 27th. Went to the drome and cleaned up a bit. Had no rain here for about 18 months and heat goes up to 127° in the shade. Had a game of fishing again, but no luck.

Two days later he flew to Broome and stayed a few days. It was at Broome that he first met Eddie Nicholson, who was to become his closest friend. Eddie was staying with his sister Rene Norman and was a junior partner in the old established law firm of Nicholson & Nicholson. His father, the Honourable John Nicholson, was a Member of Parliament.

Jimmy recorded in his diary:

> 30th. Went out to Pretty Pool shark fishing. One of the party got a swordfish about 3 feet long and shot two parrots on the

Life in the North West, 1921.

way out from the car, for use as fish bait. Any amount of these birds here, squawking all over the place. Plenty of kangaroos and turkeys to shoot at a bit further out.

November 1st. . . . There are no railways up in the north-west [there was in fact a railway line from Port Hedland to Marble Bar, but at the time Jimmy was unaware of this] everything being done by camels. Went to the picture show last night. Some show!

2nd. . . . Broome is rather a pretty place built on the block principle. It is the pearling centre and tortoise shell is found all around the coast. Landed at Hedland about 11am taking nearly five hours. Struck a very stiff wind 20 miles out.

3rd. Up again at 4.45 en route to Carnarvon. Took off at 6.00 and arrived Carnarvon 4 o'clock. Headwinds all the way and very bumpy.

4th. Dh-50. Up again at 4.45 en route to Perth . . . arrived Perth 4pm. Very nice weather. Clear. Glad to get back to a decent meal again.

Those first two months in Western Australia passed very slowly. After the initial trip north Jimmy had little to do as there were no further assignments that year. He wrote lots of letters, looked forward to receiving mail, and often went down to Fremantle to meet the mail boats — hoping, no doubt, to see a familiar face. Except for one or two pilots whom he had met, and Eddie

49

Nicholson, he knew no one. Christmas was especially lonely as his diary records:

> December 25th. This being my first Christmas Day in Western Australia I spent it very quietly. Went down to Fremantle to see the Home boat in, but did not see a soul I knew.

With the New Year, it didn't take Jimmy long to settle into a pattern of short flying stints followed by a few days leave at the particular town in which he was based. It was a rootless existence. There was no one place he could call home but he had several regular addresses — a hotel room in Perth, another in Broome, and a rented cottage in Carnarvon where he batched with Chater (a fellow pilot), and where wild goats befriended them and provided them with fresh milk. There was a freedom about the life that appealed to him. To balance this he imposed an instinctive personal discipline. His shoes were always meticulously polished, so were his buttons, and no matter at what hour he arose, and it was frequently at 4am prior to a dawn flight, he shaved. Some of his fellow pilots were inclined to scoff at his fastidiousness, seeing it as a rather quaint Scottish idiosyncrasy. For his part, Jimmy regarded some of them as slovenly.

In March 1925 Jimmy had his first real confrontation with the nature of his new job and the nature of the country where luck had landed him. On a flight south from Port Hedland he made a number of landings — at Manda, Whim Creek, Roebourne and Onslow, where he took off at 12.30pm with one passenger. He landed safely at Winning Pool, took off again and headed south, still with a single passenger. The weather turned bad. The sky grew blacker and blacker and the little plane was tossed about by the wind. Lightning flashed all around and the roar of thunder drowned out the noise of the engine. Then the engine began to overheat. There was nothing for it but to make a forced landing. Visibility by now was almost nil and Jimmy knew the danger he was in. How the passenger felt one can only imagine.

Despite the hazards, Jimmy managed to land the plane. He and his passenger were unhurt but the plane could no longer be flown. As well as the faulty engine, one of the wings had been badly damaged.

The plane had come to rest beside the telegraph line, so Jimmy tried to tap a message through the wires. He would no doubt have succeeded, except for the shocks that continually pulsed through them. Eventually a passing car took the passenger away and Jimmy slept beside the machine to await developments.

His diary for the next two weeks tells the story of his ordeal. Although he was in no danger (his position was known and assistance on the way) the problem of getting the aircraft repaired and airborne under extremely unpleasant conditions was difficult, to say the least.

Tuesday 17th March 1925. Feeling rather tired after night's sleep in the bush. My position is 120 miles south of Onslow and about 120 miles north of Carnarvon. The heat is awful and water very scarce. Mechanic Eaton came by car today. Cooked some kangaroo for breakfast.

Wednesday 18th. What an awful place of flies, they cling round in thousands all day long. Very hot today. Dismantling engine to put new blocks on. No shelter. Water rotten. The more one drinks, the more you want.

4th day. Getting rather fed up on bush life. Having nothing but bully beef and tinned goods to eat. Still very hot. Wishing I was out of here. We have got ground cleared for plane to land.

5th day. Heath came down today and brought some spares and some more bully and bread but it gets very hard with the heat. I went and got a drop of water today almost a mile away. Sandstorm blew all afternoon.

6th day. Got up and boiled the billy and had some bully and bread and butter and tea. I sleep under the tail of the bus.

Sunday 22nd. We rigged up a bit of a shelter today to keep the sun off. Writing home.

Monday 23rd. Rang [on telegraph wires] for some food to be dropped but plane continued on its journey late in the afternoon. We were very disappointed as we were out of bread. Got to work on the bully for tea. Went to bed about 10.

Tuesday 24th. Car came out from Winning Pool with supplies, which were very welcome, also we had run short of water.

Wednesday 25th. Busy with engine and Weatherell has got wing well advanced . . . Sand blowing all over the place and gets into our food. Had a good fire at night but no lamp of any

51

kind.

Thursday 26th. Got machine fairly well advanced. Some doping to be done. I went over to Mia Mia [station] in the afternoon with Adams and had an evening there and came back in the morning.

Friday 27th. Brought some water for radiator and soldering iron and gave engine a run up.

Saturday 28th. Rose early making preparations to leave but wind was in the wrong direction. About 9.30 it gradually worked round to the S.E. I took off that awful spot at 10.40 and arrived in Carnarvon at about 12.15. Very glad to get back. The engine was revving 12.75 and ran beautifully the whole way. I carried mechanics Eaton and Weatherell and their tools.

Jimmy slept in until eleven o'clock the next day, but by Monday had sufficiently recovered to go kangaroo shooting. Both he and his companion shot a kangaroo and cut off the tails to take home for soup.

There were no more forced landings that year. Jimmy had no reason to regret the rather quiet life of routine flying alternating with days of leisure — he had met Mollie.

Mollie Moseley was the adopted daughter of Mrs Moseley who ran the general store in Port Hedland and whose home was a roomy house behind the store.

Years later Mollie was to recall those days:

I called Mrs Moseley 'Darling', never 'Mother'. She was a widow. She had two sons but they were away at school in New Norcia. They were only ever home for holidays.

Everyone gravitated to the house when they came to town. All the boys from the stations. It was a very happy house. The first night I saw Jimmy was probably at Mrs Moseley's. He arrived in his Harris tweed hat and brogues and sports coat and it was as hot as could be. I thought he was quite odd because he looked so Scottish.

Mrs Moseley was important in the town. She entertained and every year she had a garden party for the station people. If there was anything social we were always invited. When the ships came in we were always asked down to have dinner with the Captain.

Mrs Moseley used to play the piano. I always thought she

played too loudly. I never liked noise. She was a large woman; rather like Queen Victoria. But full of fun. She was an asset to the town.

The house was a big bungalow type; two bedrooms and a lounge [drawing room] in the centre with verandahs all round. The kitchen was at the back. The shop ran all along the front, quite a big area. She sold everything; clothes, materials — a mixed store. There was a lot of marsh near the water. It was all mangroves then, no waterfront. There was Dalgety's, the Pier Hotel, The Esplanade (that's where Jimmy used to stay), Micklejohn's Tea Rooms, the post office, the bank, and a little vegetable shop.

I had a lot of boyfriends. Nothing serious. I loved fun. I was never a bit unhappy.

Over the next few months as he saw Mollie more frequently, Jimmy felt more and more at ease in her company but regarded her rather as he might a younger sister. She enjoyed the same things that he did; going off in the little put-put boat to the jetty and fishing; going out into the bush shooting kangaroo or wild turkey. She would ride on the back of his two-stroke motorcycle and as they ploughed through the thick sand Mollie would sometimes tumble off the bike. When Jimmy realised that he'd lost his passenger he would return to find her dusty and laughing. Mollie was to say:

The other lads didn't have a chance with me. They'd say, 'Oh, I know. Jimmy's got you.'

When Mrs Moseley began to suspect that Jimmy regarded Mollie as more than a friend she was not very pleased. She had hoped that Mollie and one of her sons might eventually make a match and did her best to discourage Jimmy's attentions. Mollie, it seemed, was unaware of any changes in the way Jimmy felt and continued to enjoy any outings he suggested.

Towards the end of 1926 Mollie broke a tooth and this gave Mrs Moseley an excuse to get her away. They would sail to Perth for dental treatment, spend Christmas in the city and return early in March. Three months separation and a busy social life in Perth would help Mollie forget her Scottish suitor, thought Mrs Moseley.

53

Probably Jimmy didn't appreciate the extent of his feelings; Mollie was always there when he was in Port Hedland. Not only was she a vivacious dancing partner, but she was game with the rifle and unflinching as she gutted fish, something he had rarely encountered in former women friends. Her lively conversation kept him amused and there was something appealing about the way she called him Jamie, a special name which no one else had used before this time. He had always been Jimmy, or Jim or Captain Woods.

When the *Bambra* sailed for Perth on 5 December 1926, with Mollie and Mrs Moseley as passengers, Jimmy discovered what it was like to be thoroughly miserable. The town seemed dull, there was nothing to do and the evenings stretched on endlessly. In his diary he wrote:

> December 6th. . . . the house is very dead no music except the old gramophone next door which gets on one's nerves.

He moped about for a week, then flights north to Broome and south to Carnarvon occupied most of his time. Christmas celebrations kept him busy too; and so the time passed.

On 17 February 1927, Mollie and Mrs Moseley returned, full of tales of the parties they had attended, the people they had met and their shopping expeditions. Jimmy and Mollie sat up talking until nearly three in the morning and he knew that she was the woman he wanted to marry. He proposed three days later and was accepted. He sent off to Perth for an engagement ring which arrived by the afternoon plane on 6 March.

'This has been one of the happiest days of my life', wrote Jimmy.

Mrs Moseley did not attend the wedding and Jimmy almost didn't make it either. The ceremony was scheduled for 8pm on 4 June 1928 at the Police Station in Port Hedland, but when Jimmy flew in that morning there was a message waiting for him. The relief pilot had made a forced landing and wouldn't be able to take over for the flight north. Jimmy had to fly on and hope that he would be back in time. The ceremony couldn't be postponed because the newlyweds were to fly to Perth the following day in readiness for their honeymoon trip to England.

Although he cut it pretty fine Jimmy was back in Port Hedland by 8pm and the wedding went ahead as planned. The ceremony

Mrs Moseley, Jimmy and Mollie, Port Hedland, 1927.

was performed by the local policeman with the resident doctor, Dr Davies, and his wife as witnesses.

As if there hadn't already been sufficient complications, Jimmy had another unexpected commitment immediately after the wedding celebrations. Mollie, recalling her wedding night many years later, said:

> ... four flying boats had arrived that day from England, so you can imagine the excitement. RAF, it was, and they were breaking the record. Jamie had to go to a party for them, so we were married and off Jamie went. We had to be up at 4 o'clock the next morning to fly down to Perth. We were there for about a week then we caught the *Narkunda* to England and we had nine months up with his people in Scotland. I think they thought I was going to be a little black girl because Jamie had said he was marrying a native of Western Australia.

Jimmy's family had moved from Udny Station to Bieldside, a suburb of Aberdeen, and the house (also named 'Arawa') was smaller than the Post Office house, which had given Mrs Wood and Jean an excuse to get rid of Jimmy's propeller chandelier. When he discovered it missing he spent days walking from auction room to antique shop, but it was never recovered.

Mollie contracted pneumonia while they were in Scotland and

nearly died. As she lay in bed, thinking of the hot sun and blue skies of Australia, and staring at the bare branches of the trees outside, it began to snow. She had never seen snow before and watched, fascinated as the flakes floated down. Years later the experience was still vivid:

> I begged them to bring me a bowl of snow to put my hands in.
> It was the most wonderful experience.

Mollie had still not recovered fully when Jimmy received a cable from Norman Brearley, recalling him. At first the doctor refused to allow Mollie to go, saying that any excitement or change of atmosphere would jeopardise her recovery. She remembers telling Jimmy, 'If you don't take me, I will die. You've got to take me.'

She was so determined it was decided that she should risk the journey. Jimmy rugged her up in blankets and they took the train to London and then went on to join the ship. By the time they reached Gibraltar and the sun, Mollie had recovered though she had lost a lot of weight. 'I was so small, they used to call us Captain Woods and the little chip. I was about six stone.'

Flyers, traditionally, are always on the move. In the early days of the industry, the nature of the job was more unpredictable than it is today, when pilots can work from and return to a fixed base, even though that base might change from time to time. Essentially, the pilots of the 1920s and 1930s were itinerants, rolling stones, and this certainly added to their aura of glamour.

For many pilots, marriage changed the nomadic pattern of life, offering a stabilising influence. For others, marriage became an encumbrance and relationships were fractured, sometimes through divorce, sometimes simply by the partners pursuing parallel lives.

When Jimmy married, his pattern was already well-set. He rarely stayed in any one place for long and had never really experienced the trauma of having to uproot himself from a firmly established base. He was not acquisitive, either; he did not hanker for possessions or property and now, with marriage, he found that Mollie shared his philosophy. Neither wanted to be tied down by the responsibilities of home ownership. They decided also, quite early in their marriage, that with the lifestyle they had chosen, they would not have children. There were no doubt several reasons for this decision, but certainly one was the risky nature of Jimmy's job and the knowledge that many colleagues had perished. Above all, both he and Mollie felt that children would change a relationship they found satisfying and adequate. As a result, Jimmy found a partner who brought a new dimension to what had been essentially a lonely life but its pattern did not undergo any radical change. He always had been, and would continue to be, a loner. He got on well with people, and was well liked, but rarely became very close to them. Even with his fellow pilots, there was no real intimacy. In fact he seemed more at home with those who employed him — Major Brearley and later, Horry Miller. This may have reflected his own vision of himself and where he felt he fitted in the social system.

It was during this period that some of the characteristics that were to mark Jimmy's style as a pilot first became apparent. He was quite prepared to take the law into his own hands if necessary, unwilling to waste time waiting about for instructions, especially if he suspected they would require him to act in a way he didn't especially want. His unorthodox actions usually endeared him to his passengers, but would have horrified Norman Brearley had he known; and as far as the authorities were concerned, his approach would probably have cost him his licence.

On one occasion, if the inscription Jimmy made on the back of a photograph of a Bristol aircraft is to be believed [see page 000], Jimmy seated a passenger on each of the plane's wings, their legs dangling over the leading edge, and their hands grasping the flying wires. They had missed the boat to Singapore in Derby and were desperate to catch up with it in Broome. With all the passenger seats booked, it was the only solution Jimmy could offer.

'It's only an hour's flying and we'll be landing at Broome', he said. 'With good weather you'll enjoy it.'

Jimmy would go to almost any lengths to help people. Once, learning that the doctor in Port Hedland had prescribed medication for a patient in Marble Bar and that there seemed to be no way of getting the medicine to the train which ran between the two towns in time, he offered to ride out on his motorcycle to intercept it.

He could also be relied upon to get prescriptions made up in

Jimmy with the Bristol. X marks where extra passenger sat.

BRISTOL. NOR. WEST PLANE 240 H.P WATER. COOLED WITH SPARE
4 GAL WATER TANK ON. TOP. WING. ON. OCCASIONS WITH. OVER
BOOKING OF PASSENGERS BETWEEN. DERBY & BROOME AND
WITH ONLY 2 SEATS INSIDE CABIN (OPEN. BOTH. SIDES) I GAVE THE
2 EXTRA PASS THE CHOICE OF SITTING ONE ON EACH. WING
MARKED X WITH THEIR. LEGS. OVER THE LEADING EDGE OF WING
AND DANGLING DOWNWARDS. AND GRASPING WITH. THEIR.
HANDS WHICH CAN BE SEEN GOING UPWARDS AND OUTWARDS
THE FLYING WIRES, AND (AFTER ASSURING THEM THEY
COULD NOT BLOW OFF A THE SLIPSTREAM WOULD
KEEP THEIR LEGS HARD ON TO LEADING EDGE OF
WING, AND THAT. IT WAS ONLY AN. HOURS. FLYING
WHEN WE WOULD BE LANDING IN. BROOME. AND WITH.
THE WEATHER GOOD YOU WILL ENJOY IT.
ANYHOW THEY HAD MISSED THEIR SINGAPORE BOAT AT
DERBY AND WERE. FORTUNATE IN. BEING ABLE TO CATCH. UP
WITH. IT AGAIN. AT. BROOME

Message written on the back of photograph above.

Perth and to deliver them, along with hard-to-come-by news-papers. Inevitably he earned a reputation as a trouble shooter: when planes were forced down or lost he was prepared to spend days, even weeks, repairing them or flying long hours in search operation.

Apart from appreciative passengers, and those for whom Jimmy did good turns, he had other supporters. One, it seems, was an aborigine, known as 'Tiger', employed as an assistant by WA Airways in Broome. An article in the *West Australian* gives some indication of the high regard in which Jimmy was held. It also gives some insight into the attitudes of the times:

> Were sparking plugs to be cleaned, hangar to be swept, or petrol laboriously pumped, 'Tiger' regarded it as his own particular job and resented interference from other hands . . . the meticulous care he exercised in keeping the curious away from the planes was the cause of amused satisfaction among the pilots. 'Tiger' regarded the pilot [Woods] in the light of a demi-god who flew through the air like some fabulous creature. Because he had flown in an aeroplane with his mentor 'Tiger' placed himself in a different mental sphere from his other coloured brothers and did not fail to show it . . . The pilot remained his hero . . . when word came that the airman was to be transferred, 'Tiger' became depressed and ill at ease and made overtures, clumsy, though sincere, to accompany his 'boss'.

At the end of March 1929, Squadron Leader Charles Kingsford-Smith, flying the Southern Cross, was lost in rugged country in the West Kimberley and Jimmy became involved in the protracted search operation.

'Smithy', with three crew — Flight Lieutenant CTP Ulm, HA Litchfield, navigator, and TH Williams, wireless operator — had set off from Sydney in a three-engined Fokker monoplane to attempt the Sydney-London record, hoping to cover the distance in thirteen days.

They left with high hopes and irrepressible good spirits. At 3am on 31 March it started to rain. For ten hours they flew through thunderstorms and clouds, unable to estimate their position. They eventually landed by the mangroves near the Georgia Mission in Brunswick Bay.

Meanwhile, none of this was known. *Smithy was missing.* One newspaper report described it as 'unthinkable' that he should be lost, and one of the most extensive and intense air searches began.

On Monday 1 April, a specially chartered mail plane, piloted by Jimmy Woods, left Port Hedland for Wyndham to look for the missing plane. There was almost as much publicity about this rescue bid as about the Southern Cross itself. Newspaper reports likened Woods to Charles Lindberg, even suggesting a physical likeness, and the hazards of the undertaking were highlighted. One of the particular problems was refuelling. Another report (there is no indication whether it was Jimmy's own suggestion) mentioned a proposition that bulk fuel be carried in the aircraft and hand-pumped into the tanks. Major Brearley, so the report continued, believed that there was far more danger of the petrol fumes igniting and the aircraft exploding than there was in running out of fuel, and would not consider the idea. Normal mail flights were deferred and the press emphasised the hazards of flying over unknown territory. It was impossible to land in most places, it was said, and it would be almost impossible to pick out a grounded plane in that wild country. The weather was unpredictable, too, with the risk of thunderstorms, and engine trouble was always a possibility. Though Jimmy serviced his plane as best he could while involved in the search, it was badly in need of an overhaul.

Eventually the Southern Cross was found, though not by Jimmy. The episode had its tragic side too because two of the searchers, Anderson and Hitchcock, perished after being forced down near Alice Springs.

The first thing that Jimmy did after hearing that Smithy was safe was to telegraph Major Brearley:

> Can I now have my plane overhauled. Engine has already well exceeded stipulated time?

At the subsequent enquiry, Kingsford-Smith and his crew were cleared of the suspicion of having carried out a publicity stunt and a premeditated landing, but were strongly criticised on a number of counts, particularly for not making sufficient effort to let the position of their landing be known.

Jimmy, on the other hand, was commended by one of the

witnesses for his efficient method of dropping aerial notes:

> He [Woods] shows the paper to us to keep us on the alert, then coming down very low, drops it in our midst. He does this systematically always in the same way so that we understand each other perfectly.

Jimmy emerged from the exercise with a reputation for being thorough, painstaking and quite undeterred by personal danger. He had shown, too, that quality of survival which would become apparent many times in the future. He might take risks, but they were always calculated risks. He knew what he was capable of and did not hesitate to carry out a task he believed to be within those capabilities. One could not say he was cautious — a cautious man would not have been involved in the hazardous business of flying in those early days — but the audacity, imprudence even, of flyers like Kingsford-Smith, was certainly not his style.

AIRMAIL

He was a caring sort of a bloke.

Frank Colquhoun

In 1929, in an effort to shorten the time it took for mail from England to reach the eastern states of Australia, it was proposed to establish an airmail service (which would also carry passengers) between Perth and Adelaide. Norman Brearley, on behalf of WA Airways, successfully tendered for the service with his proposal to use Hercules aircraft. He received a subsidy of 7,000 pounds for a five-year term.

One of the conditions of the contract was that mail destined for eastern Australia should be transferred from mail steamer at Fremantle to an aircraft waiting at Maylands aerodrome, and then flown via Kalgoorlie and Forrest (a small settlement on the Nullarbor Plain) to Adelaide. Mail steamers were scheduled to berth at Fremantle every Tuesday at 7am, but their actual arrival time was unpredictable. This meant that there was no certainty that a connection could be made in Adelaide on the same day.

Brearley overcame this problem by making provision for night flying, which was unprecedented in Australia at that time. The plane would leave Maylands sometime on Tuesday and fly as far as Forrest for an overnight stop. Next morning the flight would continue to Adelaide. To aid navigation, beacons were placed along the route, seventy miles apart, and huge landing lights were installed at Forrest. Brearley also provided hostel accommodation at Forrest for passengers and crew, with an evening meal, bed and breakfast.

On Sundays the route was reversed, and homeward bound mail arrived in time to catch the mail steamer departing from Fremantle on Mondays.

Jimmy was transferred to the East-West run when the service began and found it a pleasant change from the North West service with which he had become so familiar.

Not long after taking up his new appointment Jimmy heard that his former assistant, 'Tiger', was in hospital in Broome with a broken back. According to reports, 'Tiger' had never really come to terms with Jimmy's departure and was showing no interest in cooperating with the doctors or making any sort of recovery. Jimmy arranged to use his day off to fly the mail to northern ports and see 'Tiger'. The *West Australian* wrote a long article about 'humanity in the north', concluding:

> At Broome he visited the bed-ridden 'Tiger', whose eyes brightened and black face wrinkled with glad smile of recognition as his 'boss' walked in . . . Few words were spoken, but a wealth of understanding passed between them. The pilot left a little later to keep his air-mail schedule, but not before he had made inquiries to ensure that his coloured comrade would continue to be made as comfortable as possible. Jim had covered 2000 miles yet the morning after he returned to Perth he transferred to the Hercules to fly east and by that evening had covered a total of 4,500 miles flying in a week.

Frank Colquhoun and his brother Dave were employed by WA Airways as aircraft maintenance engineers at this time, and Frank remembers Jimmy as 'a very caring sort of a chap':

> I can remember, in those days, before he left the city, going out to the airfield to start on a flight, he would call at the newspaper office — either the *West Australian* or the *Sunday Times*, if it was a Sunday — and he would buy about six newspapers out of his own money, and with some of the stations he would pass over, he would fly low and toss them

out a rolled up newspaper. . . People in the towns up north would perhaps ask if he could get some special medicine. Jim would go out of his way to do these sort of things, just to take back, just to help out. He'd search around Perth for things that people wanted — small things, you know. He cared about people, very much so. Very much so.

Letters of appreciation give some idea of the warmth with which Jimmy was regarded:

29.7.30

Dear Pilot Woods,
    Very many thanks for dropping us the newspapers, it is indeed a pleasure to receive them, to say nothing of the novelty of having them dropped from the plane to us. We quite look forward to your trips, and had termed you (our pilot) for you always come low and we can see you quite well . . . .
Yours very sincerely,
F.E. Crewe.

While Jimmy was flying half-way across the country and back, he and Mollie were separated a good deal. They had moved to the George Hotel on the edge of Perth's central business district and Paddy, the Irish terrier they had acquired while living in Port Hedland was housed there too. Living in the hotel was a good arrangement because Mollie was free to join Jimmy whenever possible without having to leave a home untended. It also meant that she had few of the responsibilities of a young wife — no home to care for, no meals to cook, and, as they were childless, no children to look after. She played tennis, went bathing in the summer, joined friends at afternoon tea parties and led a very busy social life. This was in no way unusual; most women whose financial situation was secure combined home-making with social activity.

During this period, Mollie learnt to fly — not because she had ambitions to become an aviator like Amy Johnson, but because she was anxious to understand a bit more about Jimmy's career. Also it extended her and was an alternative to the usual way she filled her days.

Mollie's instructor was Eric Chater, Jimmy's colleague, whose

64

Loading the mail for Adelaide, 1930.

flying lessons she recalled with mixed feelings:

> He helped me to fly. I'd delay flying solo so that the lessons
> could continue. I'd go out to the airport and he would be
> waiting and I would say, 'Oh, I can't fly today. The sun is too
> high. It's in my eyes when I come over the hill and I won't be
> able to see what I'm doing.' And he used to say, 'You've got to
> go solo some time.' Eventually he said 'Now, come on Mollie.
> You've had enough [lessons]. You'll have to go off.' . . . He
> was a very big man and he got out of the cockpit and said,
> 'Now come on, get in'. I remember my knees going. And he
> said 'Now you've got to take off'. Without him it was so
> light . . . I took off very quickly. It must have been awful. But
> coming in to land . . . Chater said 'We were standing on the
> verandah at the aero club and we all went inside because we
> didn't think you'd land it in one piece'. I came down and I
> bumped and I went up about 30 feet and I bumped again. But
> I got down.

Mollie passed her qualifying tests a few weeks later, but she
never flew again.

The following winter she went out to Forrest for a couple of
months, and occasionally flew to Adelaide with Jimmy for a few
days of lively social life. On one occasion when she stayed at

Mollie unfolding wing while Chater looks on, Maylands, 1930.

Forrest during the summer, she found the heat unbearable:

> ... it nearly killed me. I used to lie under the bed ... we had linoleum everywhere, no carpet, and I used to have a bucket there and a fan on the other side and I used to dip the towel in the bucket and wrap it around me, and in ten minutes it would be dry, it was so hot!

Once while she was there they had unprecedented rain. After one extended deluge, the Nullarbor bloomed and Jimmy photographed her with Paddy among the pink and white and yellow flowers that had transformed the red earth into a living, moving pastel carpet.

Although Paddy had been intended as company for Mollie, he always seemed to be Jimmy's dog. While at Forrest he would wait for the arrival of Jimmy's plane, sitting on the ground, looking towards the west. No one would be able to hear the plane or see anything, but Paddy's tail would start to thump. Finally the aircraft could be seen, a far off speck. At the first sign of Paddy's signal, the cook at the hostel would get busy with the final preparations for the evening meal. Paddy would often fly with Jimmy, getting down on the floor of the cockpit under Jimmy's legs.

Mollie and Paddy among the everlastings, Forrest, 1931.

Frank Colquhoun recalls:

> I suppose Paddy has flown more hours in an aeroplane than
> any dog I can ever remember. Although I wouldn't say that
> Head Office was aware of it. Time after time I've seen him
> [Jimmy] get out and then Paddy would jump up onto the seat
> and Jim would lift him out.

Once Paddy became front page news. He caught his paw in a
dingo trap and it had become so badly infected that only the
prompt attention of an Adelaide veterinarian saved his life. Jimmy
and Paddy (with bandaged paw lifted) were photographed by the
newspapers.

There were a number of diversions while Jimmy was flying the
East-West run. A plague of rabbits following the rains threatened
the safe landing of planes on the airstrip because of burrows. For
several nights Jimmy and others laid cyanide baits, and in the
mornings gathered thousands of dead rabbits and carted them
away to be burnt in deep pits. Then came a plague of caterpillars
which munched their way through any remaining blades of grass.
The caterpillars disappeared as mysteriously as they had arrived.

The most dramatic diversion was the search for Paddy Whelan
in which Jimmy played a part.

On 22 December 1932, Whelan, a prospector, and Norman Stuckey, a geologist, left Forrest in a DH50 piloted by Harry Baker. They were said to be searching for Lasseter's lost reef and were expected to return the same day. Because of the inhospitable country there was some concern when they did not show up that evening. The following day Jimmy flew Dr Craig and Gorman and Sexton, two mechanics from Forrest, in a Hercules carrying approximately 600 gallons of petrol and oil, 50 gallons of water and provisions for a month. Jimmy recorded details of this expedition on the back of a map of the area:

> . . . We went over Mt Agnes and 50 miles north of Mt Aloysious. Searched various ranges, Mt Squires being on our starboard side coming back. After covering 350 miles we turned south-west to inspect Gypsum Lake but could not see any trace nor smoke of any sort, the visibility being poor. We returned to Forrest at dusk after 8 hours in the air.

The DH50 had developed an oil leak forcing Baker to land. He chose an old salt bed of roughly circular formation. He knew there was no water in it but didn't know how hard the surface would be. The plane touched down near the edge, which was quite hard, and ran in towards the centre. The wheels went through the surface crust and into the bog beneath, flipping the plane over onto its back. Stuckey was thrown out of the cabin and cut his head on the bracing wires. The other men escaped uninjured. Eventually they repaired the plane and Baker flew Stuckey back to Forrest, leaving Whelan in the desert awaiting rescue.

A brief note in Jimmy's diary for 28 December followed up the story:

> Baker and Stuckey arrived unexpectedly this morning [I] left for north on Hercules with supplies to drop to Whelan who is marooned in the desert.

On 4 January Baker flew back to pick up Whelan, escorted by two air force Wapitees.

In 1931 Jim Mollison established a new record for a solo flight from Australia to England. It took him eight days, 19 hours and 25 minutes. It was an achievement that captured the imagination of the public as well as aviators, and Jimmy began to show signs of restlessness. He too wanted to make a name for himself — to be part of aviation's history.

The late 1920s and the early 1930s were the years of the record breakers. Aviation offered amazing scope for daring and endurance. Yet for the many who dared, few succeeded. Some failed because their expectations exceeded their skills; others may not have had the toughness or the personality to cope with the long lonely hours in the air. Mechanical things went wrong for some or the weather proved too formidable an adversary. Those who were successful achieved fame and sometimes considerable fortune (the prizes offered for winners of air races were often quite significant sums). For these men — the record breakers — the temptation to try again and again almost invariably ended in tragedy. Some were lost without trace. Others crashed and were killed and some died less gloriously, through drink or dissipation.

So far Jimmy had not been tempted to make record-breaking flights but he realised that if he did not do something fairly quickly it would be too late. He was almost 40, an age at which most men might have thought twice about undertaking a solo flight of 7,000 miles. Yet the idea of breaking Mollison's record began to obsess him. On one of his brief stopovers in Adelaide he discussed the idea with Horry Miller, but Horry wasn't very encouraging — he was more interested in trying to persuade Jimmy to join him as co-pilot in the forthcoming Great Air Race of 1934. This race was to be part of Melbourne's Centenary celebrations, with a prize of 10,000 pounds offered by Sir Macpherson Robertson (the 'Mac' of MacRobertson Miller Airlines). Horry had written to Jimmy in March of 1933, enclosing a cutting publicising the race and suggesting that they might be able to think of some way to take part. He advised Jimmy not to tackle the Mollison record in a doubtful machine. (Jimmy was considering flying a Gypsy Moth owned by Jack Thorpe.)

April 20th 1933

I think you are much too good a pilot to waste your energies and risk your neck in an old Moth . . . don't let the desire to clean up that record carry you off your feet . . .

A week later Horry again wrote urging Jimmy to join him in the air race:

> As a pilot I have placed you on top of the list and as a man to have a machine in good order and keep it so, I fancy myself . . .

When Jimmy confirmed his interest, Horry went ahead with negotiations to purchase a second-hand Lockheed Vega.

Prior to this, in the latter part of 1932, Jimmy had been going about the necessary preparations for his challenge on the Australian-England record. Mollie, though she must have been aware of the risks involved, was quite fatalistic.

Jimmy aimed to time his flight for early in the New Year and it was decided that Mollie should sail to England to await his arrival. When she left on 13 February 1933, Jimmy still had no plane in which to make the flight, nor anyone to back him. Days stretched into weeks, and two months later, although Mollie was enjoying herself in London, she was anxious that Jimmy should get away as soon as possible to join her. For Jimmy the most serious problem was the fact that the Indian Monsoon season was drawing closer, which meant that flying would become more hazardous with thunderstorms, poor visibility and boggy ground to contend with. If something were not resolved, he would have to abandon his attempt.

On 10 May he telegraphed Jack Thorpe and accepted his offer of the Gypsy Moth. Then he completed arrangements with Joe Thorne, an American, and manager of Lake View and Star Ltd (a mining operation), to be his backer for the venture. The way now seemed open for the attempt. Only the details remained to be completed.

The next few weeks were frantic. Not only was Jimmy still flying to Forrest and back each week but he had to make re-fuelling arrangements for the trip with oil companies; baggage had to be forwarded and letters of clearance and visas obtained for foreign stops. He made his last flight from Forrest on 25 June, leaving himself just a week for the inevitable last minute preparations.

Safety precautions had to be devised. Jimmy had always been resourceful: he was also a realist. Some means had to be found to prevent him falling asleep at the controls on the long hops. He enlisted the aid of WE Coxon, a pioneer wireless engineer in Perth, who devised a novel alarm system. An ignition coil from a Model T Ford was attached to the control column of the aircraft. Should Jimmy fall asleep and relax his grip, he would get a minor electric shock. He also carried a red umbrella in case he had to bale out. And, so the story goes, he had a couple of tyre tubes around him, blown up, so that he would float if he landed in water. The alarm was probably the only device of any real use, though it is doubtful it would have been necessary. The noise, the vibration and the occasional turbulence would be enough to keep Jimmy awake. Apart from that, sheer determination would probably keep him alert.

Jimmy also had a special fuel tank fitted to the aircraft. It was so large the little Moth looked more like a flying fuel tank than a plane, but it did mean that he carried the maximum amount of fuel during long stretches between landings. He would carry a minimum of clothing — one clean shirt to wear on arrival at Croydon — and would make do with sandshoes or slippers on his feet. Food for the flight had to be concentrated: two tins of chicken extract, 8 ounces of Virol, 12 ounces of Wyndham meat extract, two bottles of malted milk tablets (a gift from his friend Don Plaistowe, a chocolate manufacturer, who also donated 2 pounds of hard chocolate), and a number of small paper toilet bags. Mrs Wimbridge, the cook at the Forrest hostel, presented him with a one pound tin of her home-made oatcakes and Mollie, before she left, had given him her little .22 revolver.

At last everything was in readiness. The Gypsy Moth had been painted and its name 'The Spirit of Western Australia' emblazoned on its fuselage.

Jimmy left Perth on 2 July 1933, farewelled by a crowd of well-wishers and a wad of good luck telegrams. His mascot, Felix the Cat, another parting gift from Mollie, dangled from the controls. He was taking a risk as far as the weather was concerned, yet, should he achieve what he was setting out to do — complete the journey to England in six days — he would be well beyond Asia before the onset of the Monsoon.

71

THE SPIRIT OF WESTERN AUSTRALIA

> The undercarriage fitting to the fuselage had sheared the bolts and pushed the wing up and caused a bit of damage ...

Jimmy Woods' diary, 1933.

Jimmy's official departure for his challenge flight was scheduled to take place from Broome on 3 July. His actual departure from Perth took place the day before at 5am. He was farewelled by a large crowd, many of whom were aghast at the prospect of such a tiny aircraft tackling such a daunting task. Jimmy was in high spirits, confident that everything would go well, and impatient to be off.

He kept to the coast on the way north, transmitting messages every hour. Visibility was good and the engine ran well. Shortly after passing Onslow he noticed that the engine was overheating. Then the oil pressure dropped and he was forced to land. It was hardly an auspicious beginning. Jimmy landed safely in the dark (it was then 8.45pm) and worked all night to remove the cylinder head and fit a new one.

Meanwhile in Broome there was mounting concern as Monday wore on and no news had come through of his whereabouts. It was known that he had passed over Carnarvon at 3.30pm Sunday but nothing further had been heard. Rene Norman, writing to her brother Eddie Nicholson, conveyed some of the anxiety of the waiting crowd:

July 7th 1933

> . . . we tried every possible means from this end to raise
> Hedland and as you know had everything in order here
> should he arrive — we grew steadily more anxious as the day
> wore on . . . we gave up hoping at 2am and returned home
> leaving flares burning as the moon by then had gone down . . .
> we turned in listening more or less for any sound that might
> be Jamie . . . by Wednesday the constant feeling of ears
> attuned for the drone of the engine was again with us . . .
> Jamie [finally] appeared like a star coming through the skies
> — the moon was still well up and he made a perfect landing,
> we were delighted to see his cheery old face . . .

Technically, Jimmy should not have been flying at night.
According to Visual Flight Rules he was confined to daytime
flying and should also stay clear of cloud at all times, keeping at
least 500 feet away from any cloud formation. Of course these rules
were not always observed. Pilots were caught in storms and battled
through with minimum or nil visibility, and they flew at night,
relying on the moon, the stars, and recognisable landmarks,
hoping they would not be forced to land.

Jimmy left Broome shortly after midnight on 7 July, from Cable
Beach. The plane was so heavily loaded that it would not have been
able to get off the short length of the regular strip. The beach
surface was illuminated by a string of car lights, and watchers held
their breath as the little plane laboured along the rock-hard sand.
Norman Brearley was there watching, tight lipped, but confident.

> The plane and Jamie gracefully within 400 yards rose and
> circled with its tiny guiding light into the sky, turning back
> and heading for Cape Leveque — The crowd cheered and
> sang as he got into his plane and off . . .

wrote Rene Norman.

Jimmy kept a record of his flight in a crumpled notebook, the
writing at times almost illegible because of the bumpy conditions.
He made his first entry soon after taking off:

> July 7th 2am. Leaving the coast, oil pressure 40, have just
> passed Scotts Reef. Water breaking, heavy rains. There is no

73

Take-off and arrival. 'The Spirit of Western Australia', 1933.

sign of land. Clouds too low. Four pints of oil needed. What a cow of a morning!

7.55. Visibility very bad. Another pint of oil.

11.10. Over large town. Tons of bananas. Would land for some but all paddocks are only 2 x 3, chiefly rice.

6.20. Landed at Batavia and retired to bed at 10pm.

He slept briefly, snatching only a couple of hours before leaving Batavia at 11.30 am Java time. It was raining and continued to rain as he flew on towards Sumatra.

2pm. Looks very black ahead. The Sumatra coast covered in dense scrub.

He flew on through the night, landed briefly at Muntock and took off again at 8.25am, flying through a heavy thunderstorm up the west coast of Malaya. At 8.55pm he put down at Taiping where he spent the night, taking off before dawn the following morning and heading north through twisters (unpredictable wind gusts) around the mountain peaks, thick fog and heavy rain.

Jimmy had never really experienced conditions like these before. Although he had encountered Monsoons on the North West run in Western Australia, and had been forced to land many times, it had been terrain that he knew well, with few, if any, real mountains. Here in South-East Asia, he knew nothing of local conditions; mountain peaks were a hazard and storms far more severe than any he had previously come across. Yet apart from the occasional entry 'it has been an awful day' he made little comment. The fact that he was into his second day and was already behind schedule did not seem to concern him unduly.

He landed at Victoria Point, Burma on 9 July, stopping only briefly before taking off again. Then his troubles really began. Shortly after take-off, he ran into a Monsoon. His propeller was damaged by rain, the air speed indicator blocked out and he could not climb over the ranges for fog. He was forced to return to Victoria Point where he spent the day.

Unwilling to waste time he decided to interview the Governor in order to get permission to go through Thai territory. To reach the Governor he had to cross the gulf to Thailand (then Siam).

July 10th. . . . I crossed the water in a Chinese sampan.

Encountered terrific monsoon. Our sail was up, also our umbrellas, but we were soaked. Everything was blotted out all the way across. We met a Mr Gow, an Australian manager of a tin mine . . . We were to return in a launch belonging to the miner, but the tide went out too fast and we were grounded, so had to abandon it and take the sampan in the dark . . .

He finally left Victoria Point, passing over Thailand before crossing the mountains and over Burma once more. He would jot down cryptic notes in flight and elaborate later when the opportunity arose, so that '12.50 July 11th. Very heavy rain. Crossing the mountains into Burma', becomes:

July 11th. Leaving Siam to cross mountain range. Very heavy clouds and rain meant having to fly blind for two and a half hours and only got occasional glimpses of the ground. On nearing the coast I came out at Thaton, then altered course for Rangoon. A lot of people came down to meet me . . . Did not see much of the town as it was teeming with rain when I was landing.

Four days gone! Jimmy must have realised by this time that there was no real hope of finishing the journey within the planned time. It was now very unlikely that he would be able to match the record, let alone break it. But he showed neither impatience nor disappointment. The flight itself had become the most important thing. The weather had proved more formidable than he had ever anticipated.

He took off for Calcutta on the morning of 12 July and flew about 130 miles before he discovered that the gravity tank pump was not working. To put it more bluntly, the petrol pump had failed and he was forced to turn back.

July 12th. . . . not having enough [petrol] to reach Rangoon I looked around for a spot to land on. The whole country being flooded, and all the area paddy and rice fields, which covered about 25 yards each roughly, with walls of mud built around each, that was no good, so I picked out an island in the middle of the river and it was small and very boggy, and in 2 minutes about 2,000 Burmese swarmed across the river in all sorts of boats and they were an awful job to control as they had never

77

seen an aeroplane except flying high and I had to threaten them with a big spanner. One fellow threw a lump of mud at my machine and I threw the spanner at him, which caught him on the foot as he was running. He didn't come back. After that the police arrived and took control. Then the District Commissioner came sailing up the river in his yacht and asked me over to have some lunch and I was soaked to the skin, so he gave me a change of clothing and a pair of wellington boots and all afternoon it simply teemed down and as the river was rising a foot a day, and only one more foot to go before it would have reached my machine, we worked frantically to get aloft after dumping 70 gallons of petrol onto the ground, which some fool put a match to and it was a beautiful blaze. Several attempts to get off always ended up nearly going on my nose. However the last attempt I just got away with the water splashing up right over the left wing. I would just manage a landing at Bassein before dark.

Having landed safely at Bassein in spite of the soft ground, he was taken by the District Commissioner to stay with him for the night. Never was a bath and a meal more welcome. Next morning, after filling up with petrol he attempted to take off.

July 13th. I did not get far. I was bogged right up to the wheels. So, with about fifty natives, we dug her out, but every time we got the wheels out onto the planks, [and] we tried to move, we went back down to the axles and all the time it was teeming with rain, the ground being blotted out.

The weather report from Calcutta was bad, but Jimmy finally got away from Bassein on the morning of 15 July, climbing through continuous rain and heavy cloud. He reached Akyab at 9.30am where he spent the day. When he attempted to get off for Chittagong en route to Calcutta he found the magnetos soaked with water. These had to be dried and it was midday before he got the engines started.

Made good time to Chittagong through heavy clouds and rain and I decided to go through Chungpur as the storm was banking up to the west. It got very bad and I couldn't get over it, so I looked round for a landing but that was impossible so I had to return to Chittagong.

78

Jimmy's log/diary at this point took on a rather different tone. Certainly there were matter-of-fact entries relating to position and weather conditions, but more and more space was devoted to writing about people he met and his experiences on the ground.

July 19th. After leaving Chittagong I climbed to 9,000 feet to try to get over the storm . . . so I had to fly blind for about two hours and it was pouring with rain. I came down later and found there was only 30 miles to Calcutta. After filling up I pushed off for Allahabad and there was a very strong southwest wind blowing and I had to land at Gaya where there is a good aerodrome. As I brought my machine alongside the filling place a young chap came up in a big 8 cylinder Studebaker and asked if I had anywhere to stay, and I said that unless the petrol agents had arranged anything I hadn't and he took me to his father's place and to my surprise when he drew up in front of a huge mansion. I was introduced to His Highness, the Maharajah of Tekari ['Tikari], and I was quite a filthy airman, there was no doubt whatever. Well, he was just delighted to see me and there were about 50 servants around ranging from aides down through the order of secretaries and butlers to the ordinary kind. His Highness ordered tea and I was to have a car, one of the 15 he possesses, ranging from Rolls, Lancias, Mercedes-Benz, Studebaker, Buicks and goodness knows how many other makes. So an Englishman and I set out afterwards in the Buick to the station to get a tarpaulin to put over my machine, then out to the drome, which is about 6 miles out.

Then we came back and the Maharajah ordered more tea. Afterwards I had a bath and a clean up. Then I met a few High Court judges and celebrities. We sat down to dinner about nine. Had great feast. I can feel my mouth now, as the curry was so hot, but good. He [the Maharajah] was in the air force during the war so was quite interested in my maps and my flight generally from Australia. The mosquitoes are quite bad tonight, but I have a net and a fan over my bed. I see new servants every 5 minutes. Goodness knows how many he has. He and his son and party shot four tigers the other day, apparently quite numerous round here. I just hope they won't take a mouthful of my machine during the night. If they smell Mrs Wimbridge's oatcakes, they might go off. To bed now, 10.30.

After such hospitality it was something of an anti-climax to be back once more in the air. Three hours after take-off, just after crossing the Ganges near Benares, Jimmy noticed that the cockpit was flooding with petrol. There was no hangar at Allahabad so he risked flying on to Lucknow where he found a hangar in the aero club.

> . . . they helped me to take my big tank out. Had the whole centre section to remove. Also take bent pins of wings out and a very big job. Found a split in the tank 6 inches long, so we put a plate on, well soldered and will finish the job at 2am.

While Jimmy was preoccupied with the difficulties of his flight, Mollie was uncertain of his whereabouts. Occasionally a very short report would appear in the English newspapers, giving quite noncommittal information about his progress. There was little indication of how very difficult the flight had proved, nor was there much mention of its dangers. Mostly, the reports stressed that he was running well behind schedule.

The next couple of days passed uneventfully as Jimmy continued his flight across India, although the authorities at Jodphur tried to stop him going on to Karachi as the drome there was unserviceable. He managed either to talk his way out of that or simply ignored it. Karachi, whose average annual rainfall was only 5 inches, had already had 15 inches in one week and the ground was decidedly boggy. Jimmy landed safely.

> What a sight Karachi is after the rain, thousands of mud huts washed away or roofs fallen in. Roads all washed away. Everybody, of course, was expecting a crash [when he landed]. I found also my permits for Greece, Italy and France had not turned up . . . cabling London today . . .

Lack of permits didn't appear to cause Jimmy much concern. He worked on the principle that if he landed at one of the foreign airports without a permit, they couldn't do much about it, and once there he would be able to talk his way out of any awkward situation.

After leaving Karachi, Jimmy headed out over the sand dunes and along the coast of the Gulf of Oman. Visibility was reduced because of haze, and the weather was warming up. All went well until he reached Bandar Abbas in Iran (then Persia). He had already been forced to land at Jaske for a Customs check and spent an hour as they fussed over quarantine. No one would come near him in case he was infectious and he had to put his fee of one pound on the ground with a stone over it before the doctor would accept it.

> July 27th. Heat here awful. Police come and go. Went out to dine with Mr Chapman and also a German Bank Manager, Mr Hoffer. They are the only Europeans here apart from the Consul who is away at his summer residence about 300 miles from here where it is cooler. I am getting Persian food, which I am not very fond of, but I drink plenty of tea all day long. The water is not too good.

It took some time to convince the authorities that his passports and permits were in order but eventually Jimmy prepared to take-off for Basra. He looked over the ground which was very rough and posted two men in position for take-off.

> I opened the throttle and after about 100 yards I heard a terrible crack come from the starboard side and the machine tilted to one side, so I cut the throttle, thinking it was only a puncture, but when she came to a standstill I knew something worse had happened, as the wing was scraping the ground . . . I got out and had a look. The undercarriage fitting to the fuselage had sheared the bolts and pushed the wing up and caused a bit of damage, but repairable . . . sent a telegram to Wakefields, Karachi, to send a spare piece by Dutch or French mail plane, and to get them to drop it when passing. If they won't do that it will have to come by steamer which will take over a week.

Reading between the lines one can sense the frustration. Here he was, stuck in a remote part of Iran, able to communicate only by cable or telegram, uncertain whether his messages would be understood, or even if they would be received. He was ill-equipped for the extreme heat, he hated the food, and there were only two people with whom he could converse. Yet he never questioned that the parts would arrive, it was only a matter of when. With growing impatience he recorded the passing of the next 12 days.

> 29th. Banderabbas [Bandar Abbas]. Still waiting for a reply to

my telegram to Karachi asking if spare parts can be sent by French or Dutch planes and dropped here, but like everything else in Persia, things move slowly. The people have no inclination to hurry or try anything modern. Went out to dinner last night to Hoffer's place. Chapman was there too, and tonight I am going to Chapman's. They are the only whites here. The Persian food tastes very strange. They bake great discs of brown-looking bread, which is more like a piece of sugar bag than bread. Time is passing very slowly but hope to move once I do get going.

4.30pm. Just had some tea and no milk so I squeezed lemon into it and also brought from my tucker box in the plane some of Mrs Wimbridge's oatcakes which she made before I left and, my word, I did enjoy them. Just had the police in for my passport again. They are very annoying at times.

Sunday 30th July. Another day passes slowly. Had a reply from Karachi saying the French mail plane would bring the parts on Wednesday, but would possibly have to carry them on to Lingeh which is over a hundred miles past here and with no means of communication, so I replied it was essential they drop them here. I had a look at the beach yesterday and I think I could take off light and land there to fuel up. It would be easier on the machine.

31st July. 7.30. Just been over to the beach to see if I could wheel the machine over, but it's impossible, so I shall get some labour to clean up the ground a bit and take off light then fuel up at the beach.

Tuesday 1st August. What a heat. The perspiration is simply pouring off me today and I think I have a touch of prickly heat. Have been over the plane since 6 o'clock patching up a bit and have everything done ready for the spares, which I hope will come tomorrow, Wednesday. Had a wire from Karachi today saying they would make every endeavour to persuade the pilot of the French plane to drop them. I shall be very glad to take off from this awful place of sand and dust and flies. It's awful. I was having a rest this afternoon when a message arrived from Mr Hoffer asking me if I would like to go out to the German steamer which had just arrived from Germany and the various Gulf ports with sugar etc. . . They had excellent beer but my drink was only a squash. Then we had a splendid dinner, I really enjoyed it. Then we left about twelve for the port and I was sorry to leave the ship knowing I had to come back to this sandy hole. However, I was soon asleep when I did get to bed.

Wednesday 2nd. . . . am now waiting for the French mail plane.

Thursday 3rd July. Another day wasted. Just discovered one of the tyres had a leak, so pulled it off this morning and repaired it. Got a telegram from Karachi this morning saying the French plane delayed at Calcutta and that the parcel would be dropped from the Dutch plane Saturday or Sunday. This hanging around with such uncertainty is awful, and nowhere to go. Will be glad to get back to civilisation and good food.

Friday 4th July. Another day gone. This is the Persian Sunday so all is quiet as on most days. Humidity is terrible at times . . ., often I have just only a towel around me.

Saturday 5th August. . . . the continued uncertainty is not too good for one's temper, but what can one do but wait. Went out for a run with Hoffer in his Ford which helped to pass the time a bit, then at night we all met at his place for dinner.

Sunday 6th. Was up early waiting for the hum of the Dutch aeroplane, but so far no noise. I doubt if they will come today. Think I will drop a few lines to the Major [Brearley] and Fatty [Nicholson] . . .

Monday 7th. Waited and waited all day for the Dutch plane to arrive and then a wire arrived from Karachi to say that the French mail [plane] would bring it on Wednesday. Very disappointing and it is quite a simple thing for them to do to just drop the parcel, as they go over. When I reach London I am to communicate with the General Manager of KLM . . . My word, I'll be glad when I get away from this awful country of flies, sand and heat and filth generally.

Tuesday 8th. Just a month since I left Australia, it seems years, but hope to make up for all when I arrive in London. My little Mollie will be so disappointed. This has been another awful day.

Perhaps it was as well for his own sanity, that Jimmy retained a colonial British attitude to his dilemma. By clinging steadfastly to the things he knew and understood — the company of a couple of Europeans, the logic of believing in the eventual arrival of the plane with spare parts, the resistance to foreign food — he was able to maintain a kind of confidence in a successful outcome to his journey. No good would come of dwelling on his isolation. Cables could be sent, planes did pass overhead, ships would occasionally drop anchor. There is no hint in his diary of inner doubts, or of any perception of the incongruity of his situation in a land where Iranians in flowing robes accepted flat discs of bread as norm and camels as a more legitimate mode of transport than flimsy metal birds. He would endure, or if fate intervened, he would perish, but he would never compromise. He was too much a Scot for that.

At last he got off, leaving from the beach at Bandar Abbas on 10 August. He headed for Bushire and intended to make a stop on the way at Kanjan. Fortunately there was a good beach on which to land.

> I noted the imprints of a mob of camels and they appeared not to like the ground. A great many Persians came out to meet me. I am staying with the Director of Customs and they are very hospitable. It was impossible to see anything . . . a very high wind blowing. You could not see the sunset after 6 o'clock owing to the dust. The bus is already tied down on the beach all snug with four guards attending. I shall sleep tonight all right.
>
> Friday 11th August. Dust storm very bad. I couldn't leave until low tide in the afternoon and I rode out to the plane which was one and a half miles from the village and my Arab horse tried to do a loop with me but I made him do a half roll instead . . .

For the first time during his long ordeal, Jimmy admitted to not feeling well.

He had tried to avoid Iranian food as much as possible, finding it unpalatable, but had drunk excessive cups of weak tea with lemon. Only on occasions when he had dined with Hoffer or Chapman had he eaten much at all. Now this erratic diet was having an effect and he confessed to feeling a bit weak. To stave off nausea and to ease the emptiness in his stomach, he prepared a make-shift meal of oatcakes, Wyndham extract and some malted milk tablets which he mixed with boiling water . . . 'that bucked me up a bit'.

It was more than three weeks since he had been able to have a proper bath or really enjoy a meal. Bushire proved to be a real oasis after what he had been through.

August 11th. I was very dry and hungry. I had some lemonade with plenty of ice, but I had all this in a beautiful cold bath. It was most delightful and soothing for my sunburnt limbs and I was in that bath for almost an hour. Then I had a lie down for a bit until dinner time and just wrapped a sheet around myself for that.

Saturday 12th August. Had a good night's sleep and after a shower had some fried eggs and bread and butter and Australian jam (Rosella). Quite a treat. Ishmael. Dust storms on this morning. Can't see the houses owing to the storm. I may get away to Basra this afternoon, should it clear. Ormuz held up way down the Gulf for the same reason. Just going to have a cup of Wyndham extract.

Sunday 13th August. Depart Bushire. The machine is full of red ants. They are crawling over everything . . . Didn't see the ground for two and a half hours, owing to sand storm.

Later that day Jimmy landed at Baghdad having battled against headwinds all the way. It was very hot when he landed, but his reception by the authorities more than made up for the heat. Customs was cleared quickly and he was accommodated

. . . in a splendid hotel and was soon provided with nice iced lemonade and lunch. Then I went over to the hangar and did some maintenance on my engine and got some coolies to clean the bus down as she was in a very dirty state, about a quarter inch of dust. After dinner, which by the way, was one of the best I have ever had (I would like to stay here for a week). The aerodrome manager took me for a run in his car through the town of Baghdad . . . a very nice city, nice gardens and boulevards.

The next day he headed for Aleppo where he once again had some difficulties over landing permits. Then his log becomes a series of place names linked to hours in the day.

11.50. Crossing Aegean Sea, very choppy.
1.00. Patmos Island.
1.50. Andros island.

And so on, over Greece, across the Adriatic, up the Italian coast and over the mountains, past Vesuvius and Naples to Rome.

In Rome he arranged for a cable to be sent to Mollie who had spent an anxious six weeks in London. Relieved that he had put her mind at rest, Jimmy flew on, skirting the Italian coast and the French Riviera.

> Might land for a shot at the tables at Monte Carlo. Over Mentone. Over Nice, Cannes, St Raphael, Marseilles, and just spotted Notre Dame. The Rhone is very pretty just now. Lyon. I nearly missed the hospital train here. On our way back from Egypt (1919) we only stopped for a short while and I wanted safety blades so ran into the nearest shop and when near the railway station I saw the train move off and I just managed to jump onto the bumper.

With the pressure off and the end in sight, Jimmy was beginning to relax and write more freely. Shortly after passing over Paris he reported that his main tank was dry but was confident that he had enough fuel to reach Croyden. He had planned to have a shave before landing, but there was some turbulence and it would soon be dark so he gave up the idea. In another hour he would reach Croyden and Mollie. The successful, if protracted flight and the end of the long separation from his wife, wiped all memory of the frustrations, discomforts, dangers and disappointments from his mind.

It was almost dark was he flew into Croyden.

'My name is Woods and I've just flown from Australia. Is my wife here?'

But Mollie was not there. His cable had never arrived. He realised later that the money for its dispatch (along with his fountain pen) must have found its way into the postal official's pocket and the message dropped into the rubbish bin. It was a bitter disappointment.

His unexpected arrival was soon picked up by the press and he was whisked away to Fleet Street for interviews, while a couple of reporters went to get Mollie.

She was staying at a private hotel in Earls Court. By the time the reporters arrived it was 3am and the proprietor, who had no idea who the men were, refused to allow his young guest to accompany them. Finally they were able to convince him that they meant no harm, that they indeed had the flyer in their office and above all else he wanted to see Mollie, his wife.

For Mollie, the memory of that reunion was as vivid nearly 50 years later as when it first happened:

> They took me out and we banged the car on the way, which didn't help very much, and by the time I got there I was a wreck. I was taken up to the night editor's room and he wanted to give me a drink. It was a whisky and I said 'Oh no thank you'. Then Jamie came in. He was terribly thin. His hair had all gone from the bumping and bumping and bumping... and all he had for luggage was a flour bag with a dingo on it... that was all he had, and of course my little gun. He wasn't supposed to have it but I made him take it, but it had rusted up. We were so happy. But that wasn't the end of it. When we got back to Earls Court I didn't have a key. I left in such a hurry. We couldn't get in and by that time it was 4 or 5 o'clock in the morning, so Jamie put me on his shoulders and I climbed up. I was always a good climber. I climbed up and pulled the window down and got in over the top of it.

Next day the papers were full of the story.

Occasionally over the previous six weeks there had been small news bulletins, a couple of lines to say that Jimmy had landed at Allahabad or was still stuck in Bandar Abbas. Now the press was able to run full columns, not only about Jimmy and his feat, but about Mollie, who was also a pilot and had waited for him. It was an exciting and heady time. Jimmy loved it. He may not have broken Mollison's record, but he was in his own way something of a hero. Up at Udny, he, Mollie and 'The Spirit of Western Australia', stripped of paint after the battering she had endured, received an enthusiastic welcome.

1934: THE GREAT AIR RACE

Jimmy was quite unperturbed . . . an undercarriage leg jammed solid and nothing we could do would move it. Even this did not interefere with Jimmy's tranquility.

D.C. Bennett.

Jimmy and Mollie had a great reunion with family and friends in Scotland, their own months of separation forgotten. During that time, in numerous press interviews, Jimmy declared that he intended to fly back to Western Australia, but in a larger machine — if that were not available, then certainly in the Gypsy Moth. But the return flight did not eventuate — Jimmy received an urgent cable from Norman Brearley requesting that he return immediately. He and Mollie sailed for Australia on the *Strathnaver* early in October and the Moth was shipped back separately.

Jimmy's taste for leisure was well and truly satisfied after a few weeks of shipboard life. Within hours of his return in November he was off to Forrest, back into the routine of flying the East-West route and Mollie moved back into their room at the George Hotel.

The disappointment over his unsuccessful challenge of Mollison's record did not deter Jimmy from considering other ventures — you tackled something, you did your best and that was the end of it. No recriminations; no regrets. Look ahead to the next challenge — and now, always at the back of his mind was the goal of the

Welcome in Aberdeen, 1933. Charles and Elizabeth Wood with Jimmy and Mollie.

Centenary Air Race from London to Melbourne.

Although he was not an ambitious man in the usual sense of the word, there lurked in James Woods a dare-devil quality which he managed to conceal beneath a low-key, laconic manner. He was not flamboyant or reckless. He was neither a drinker nor a womaniser, qualities that earned some of the trail-blazers in aviation considerable limelight. Yet he did seem to attract publicity of a less notorious kind. The press treated him well and he earned a great deal of public esteem. He enjoyed this enormously and could always be relied upon for a good-natured interview and some photographic coverage.

He and Horry Miller still planned to fly together in The Great Air Race of October 1934. The plane, a Lockheed Vega, had been bought and they had managed to interest a sponsor — David Robertson, Sir MacPherson Robertson's brother. (It would not have been appropriate for 'MacRobertson' to sponsor his partner, because he had already put up the 10,000 pounds prize money.)

Although breaking records was something that challenged aviators, the race was aimed at more than record breaking. MacRobertson was anxious that contestants heed safety factors and that the race prove that it was possible to provide a quicker link between Britain and Australia for passengers and freight.

WA Airways' contract for the North West airmail service was due to expire in 1934. Tenders had been called for the new contract and Norman Brearley submitted his with reasonable confidence that it would be accepted.

At this time Horry Miller's Commercial Aviation Company (which had been renamed MacRobertson Miller Airlines after Sir MacPherson Robertson became a financial partner) was facing a crisis. The company had been forced to sell 'Old Gold' its flagship (ironically, it turned out, the sale was to WA Airways) to pay wages, and there was the possibility that other planes in the fleet would also have to go. Horry Miller was very despondent about the position of the company.

At about this time, Jimmy was on one of his stopovers in Adelaide and he and Horry sat up half the night discussing the feasibility of MMA tendering for the North West contract. It was well known that the subsidy which WA Airways had received in the past was 2 shillings and sixpence a mile. Horry, having already discussed the matter with his accountant Bob Patterson, considered it possible to provide the service for one shilling and sixpence a mile. He also said that, should he win the contract, he would like Jimmy to become his route manager. He could offer 20 pounds a week and a retirement package based on the number of weeks service with the company. Jimmy indicated that he was interested, but nothing was written down. Years later, he wrote, in a draft letter for his lawyer:

> Captain Miller and I were friends of fairly long standing and my training and make up is such that I would have regarded it as showing no confidence in Captain Miller's word had I requested that the arrangement be recorded in some formal manner.

And again, years later, this was something Jimmy was to regret. MMA did submit a tender and some weeks later was informed that

90

it had been awarded the contract for the North West airmail service. This meant that it would be quite impossible for Horry Miller to go off to England to compete in The Great Air Race. Jimmy could still go, and fly the Vega, but he would have to find someone else as navigator.

For Norman Brearley, losing the contract meant that WA Airways operations were halved and there would have to be drastic cut-back in staff. Jimmy's voluntary move to MMA saved them both some embarrassment, though there was a hint that relations had not always been entirely harmonious. Writing to Mollie shortly before the start of The Great Air Race, Jimmy said:

> ...I do feel sorry for Norman ... one of the best fellows in the world when away from aeroplanes and hangars, especially Perth ones. We are excellent pals still.

For Jimmy Woods, 1934 looked like becoming a year of real challenge: the Air Race in October and route manager for MMA upon his return. But there was still a great deal to be done. Licences had to be renewed and taxation clearances obtained and Jimmy had to undergo a medical examination. The question of co-pilot or navigator still had to be resolved and he needed to get a Certificate of Airworthiness for the Vega, something that could involve protracted work on the machine in Holland. He planned to travel to England via the United States in order to visit the Lockheed Company and find out as much as he could about the Vega and the spare parts that might be required.

Jimmy's last trip was on Wednesday 13 June 1934 from Forrest to Adelaide. If he felt sentimental about leaving the service he did not betray it in his diary; his last entry was to the point, recording take-off and landing times and a cryptic: 'Last trip with Airways'.

Jimmy and Mollie spent a few days in Adelaide, then went on to Melbourne by train. While Jimmy was away this time, Mollie would stay in Melbourne, spending her time partly with Colonel Jess and his wife, and partly with David Robertson and his family. Jimmy put his luggage on board the *Monterey*, intending to join the ship in Sydney. That way he could spend the weekend with Mollie and attend to some business in Sydney before sailing for the United States on Wednesday 27 June.

There was never anything leisurely about Jimmy's departures.

He rarely seemed to allow enough time to do all that had to be done, yet he never panicked; quietly — stolidly perhaps — he dealt with each item or crisis as it arose. Fortunately Mollie was not a worrier: she accepted the way Jamie chose to run his life and never interfered. For his part he allowed her an unusual amount of freedom for the times. Their relationship was one of mutual trust, a letting go, that in its way ensured that though often apart, essentially they remained together.

Jimmy had a busy time in America, sightseeing, visiting Lockheeds at Burbank, going up in an airship and flying in a Curtiss Condor from Detroit to New York; he surveyed that city from the top of the Empire State Building and marvelled at its 102 floors. On 28 July he sailed on the *Britannic* for England.

The first thing Jimmy did on arrival was to go to Australia House to get 'my darling's mail', and to catch up with Eddie Nicholson who was also in London. Then he had to get to work. He dashed out to Harnsworth aerodrome to look at the Vega and found that there was a great deal to be done — amongst other things the tail unit and the ailerons were off, which kept him busy for the next few days. He also had to get Air Ministry sanction to fly the plane to Holland.

After a week of working on the aircraft Jimmy was able to test it and found it handled well. He fitted in a visit to The Oval to watch a Test Match and spent a week with his family in Aberdeen.

On his return to London, Jimmy visited Norman Brearley and his wife, then continued to rush round finalising details for the race; this included getting the paint stripped, the plane sprayed with undercoat and then finished in cream cellulose with a red line and registration.

In a letter to Mollie dated 13 September, he gave a lively description of an evening with Jim Mollison:

> Mollison drove me back to town in one of the new Buicks and my word I was glad when I got out. We passed everything, he dodged in and out using one of those sirens like the police have and would get up to 55 m.p.h. and get right up behind a car and suddenly jam all his brakes on. Ye Gods. Well, when we left the drome we only got about two miles when he had to stop at the first hotel just to have a short one. Then on again for about another two miles, and another, and at this one

some dame recognized him and brought an envelope for him to autograph. I could see what was going to be the outcome so I said I was sorry I would have to hurry as I had an appointment in town at 9.15 . . .

. . . My word I wouldn't drive with him again for £20,000.

Jimmy still did not have a co-pilot for the race and with little over a month to go, the situation was getting desperate. Then he heard that Flight Lieutenant DC Bennett had been unable to get a suitable aircraft to enter the race in his own right. It seemed almost too good to be true. He contacted Bennett and proposed that he should fly as navigator in the Vega. With negotiations completed, Woods and Bennett were officially entered as competitors number 36. There were 19 other contestants.

Bennett considered the Vega a good aeroplane but thought the preparation had been hurried. In his book *Pathfinder* he described some of the problems:

> . . . Jimmy Woods was obviously harassed by lack of sufficient funds to do things properly. The aircraft was secondhand, and he arranged for a number of modifications and other work to be carried out. On the day we should have arrived at Mildenhall, the starting point, the aircraft was still not complete, but late that afternoon we managed to take off [to test the plane]. In spite of the late hour, Jimmy was quite unperturbed. In fact even while we still had time to reach Mildenhall, he went to the phone, telephoned through to the race committee, and got permission to arrive one day late at the assembly point. It was fortunate that he did, as an undercarriage leg jammed solid and nothing we could do would move it. Even this did not interfere with Jimmy's tranquility.

Jimmy's account was more brusque. In his diary he wrote:

> Monday 15th October. Undercarriage stuck on landing [at Heston from Harnworth]. Worked all day and got away to Mildenhall just before dusk, landing there in the dark.

Jimmy kept a cutting of a newspaper report (undated and unidentified) of his late arrival:

> He [James Wood] was the fourteenth competitor to reach

Mildenhall . . . He had to arrive today to be eligible for the race.

Officials had given up hope of his arriving tonight. They were about to close the hangars when the white shape suddenly zoomed from the skies.

Officials and attendants rushed on to the aerodrome. With no preliminary circuit of the field the monoplane glided down and landed on the darkened runway.

For a few moments it appeared that taxiing fast, Woods might overrun the edge of the aerodrome, but he managed to pull up with only feet to spare from the stone walls of the hangars.

The slight figure in soft hat and short raincoat grinned cheerfully from the cockpit.

'That was certainly a moment,' he said. 'Just as I was coming down I saw what looked like a giant sausage in front of me. I only just managed to pull over it. It was too dark for me to see what it was.'

The week before, on 22 October, the Royal Aero Club had turned on a grand banquet in honour of the race and its pilots. It was a dressy occasion at Grosvenor House in Park Lane, with the men in smart uniforms or black tie and the women wearing formal gowns. There were more than 500 guests.

The day before the start of the race, hordes of people converged on Mildenhall. They gazed at the aeroplanes, marvelling that some of these flimsy machines were capable of the long flight. The pilots were the centre of attention; and the gathering of so many idols, forerunners of film and pop stars — Amy and Jim Mollison, Parer, Scott, Black, Roscoe Turner (carrying a lion's tail), Jacqueline Cochran (befurred and wearing an orchid) — created enormous excitement. The unexpected arrival of King George V, Queen Mary and the Prince of Wales brought even more chaos. Roscoe Turner greeted the King with 'Hullo King' which amused everyone, while his invitation to the King to look inside his aeroplane caused some dismay; it was well known that the King wasn't a bit interested in flying and hated aeroplanes. People partied all night and many turned up at the starting point in evening dress to watch the beginning of the race the next morning.

The pilots, many of whom had slept in their cars, had a quick

Mildenhall: the start of The Great Air Race, 1934.

breakfast before heading for their machines. Mechanics had already started up some of the engines; loud speakers barked instructions; wind and weather information was being transmitted and the aeroplanes began to taxi from the hangars to the tarmac to line up in position. The excitement was electric. At this moment, a section of the crowd — some 10,000 people — surged onto the runway. Alarm swept through the pilots, dismayed in case their precious machines should be damaged, but police on motorcycles and firemen in tenders put up a show of force and the crowd fell back.

The Lord Mayor of London stood with an upraised flag ready to wave down the first machine at 6am. One of the Comets, piloted by Cathcart-Jones, took off first. The Mollisons and Roscoe Turner weren't far behind. Jimmy Woods and Don Bennett took off at 6.39, shooting away with a steep climb into cloud. They had no radio so had to rely entirely on dead reckoning. They landed at Marseilles three hours and 45 minutes later. Bennett wrote:

> . . . Jimmy Woods had implicit faith in my navigation and was under the happy delusion that a navigator could work

magic. Fortunately . . . his reliance on my navigation did not go astray. We pressed on to Rome, and thence in the dark to Athens.

They weren't sure whether they had enough range to reach Aleppo. As the only alternative was Nicosia which had no night flying facilities, they decided to get a little sleep in Athens. The Greek Air Force put them up in the local barracks and after a short nap they took off again. Bennett said later that as they were lifting off, he had the impression that the undercarriage had jammed again, as it had at Heston. This may have been hindsight, because Jimmy made no mention of feeling any uneasiness at the time.

Because Bennett was not involved in the actual landing of the plane at Aleppo, his recollection of the incident gives a slightly different perspective from Jimmy's.

Bennett wrote:

> On arrival at Aleppo, in Syria, Jimmy brought the Vega in to land whilst I took up my position as far aft as possible. He hit the ground with a fair wallop and the undercarriage collapsed; down she went, and the nose went in as we whipped over onto our back.

Bennett was flung from one end of the cabin to the other, his body concertina-ing before he rolled clear into the dust. Jimmy was still trapped inside the plane. His forehead was bleeding badly and he looked an awful mess. Bennett's knee was injured and he couldn't move his head or shoulder — three vertebrae had been crushed.

Immediately he was able, after getting clear of the plane and even before any medical assistance was given, Jimmy scrawled a note to Mollie on the back of a map of Cyprus. It was stained and dirty, but it was the only paper he could find. He gave the note to Squadron Leader MacGregor, whose Miles Hawk touched down about an hour after the Vega's unfortunate landing:

> I am so sorry for you dear, please don't worry about me. I am all right.
> . . . Luckily we did not catch fire . . .
> . . . I shall await instructions from Horry. I have not got much time as they are about to leave . . .

96

Jimmy and Bennett study the damage, Allepo, 1931.

After being taken to a nearby convent and patched up by some Syrian nuns, Jimmy arranged for a cable to be sent to Mollie:

21st October 1.10am
Regret undercarriage collapsed Aleppo. Machine out of race.
Inform D. Robertson and Horry.
Love Jamie

He wrote a much longer letter that night to David Robertson.

Dear Mr Robertson,
... Well this has been a sad day for us all and I would have sooner lost a limb than see such a beautiful machine wrecked and I cannot tell you how I sympathise with you for your loss. There was nothing like it at Mildenhall and it was a pleasure to pilot.

... We made a good three pointer and after running along a bit I was just preparing to draw up with the brakes when down she went on one side, the wing tip touched and over she went on her back with a crash. Luckily I switched the engine off and my main battery switch which I think probably prevented a flare-up. I rolled around the cockpit and hot oil pouring all over my head, I realised it was time to be outside but could not open the cockpit door and the roof exit of course was on the ground. Bennett was already outside shouting was I all right so after a bit of pressure I forced open the door. He was sitting at the rear of the cabin when she went over and got thrown forward. He had a nasty gash in his leg and I got one on the forehead ... apart from a few bruises we are quite O.K. But . . . it was plain the poor old Vega was badly wounded. The impact of the engine on the ground burst all the mountings and also pushed in the front of the metal fusilage which is badly sprung. The port wingtip is also gone including a piece of the spar, the fin is only slightly damaged.

The cause of it all being the radius strut on the port side of the undercarriage breaking right in the middle. The undercarriage oleo leg had stuck in the OUT position several times and we had it down at Heston a few days before the race. I found the cylinder scored and worn but could not do anything with it.

... I had the machine pulled onto its wheels after repairing the strut and have it over at the military hangars. I removed most of the instruments this afternoon as they would certainly have been stolen by these thieves.

I did not mention the propellor. It is also bent but can be put right.

This is a hell of a place to be stranded in, they all talk French. Bennett leaves for London tomorrow morning via Port Said. I told him to send his passage expenses out as that was the least we could do.

It is all very regrettable and I can assure you am feeling pretty miserable tonight. However it could have been worse and we have something to be thankful for. I wrote my wife but did not tell her much and told her not to worry as I am all right.

. . . May the Vega live to see Australia.

Jimmy wrote again to Mollie the next day, concluding:

Darling, I hope you will go to all the functions and keep bright and just be the same brave little girl of old.

The next few days were awful. Jimmy, short of money, still suffering from the blow to his head, disappointed and alone in a foreign land, waited for funds from Australia, instructions from his sponsors and some reassurance from Lockheed that the Vega could be repaired, preferably in Australia. Most of the race entrants had passed through Aleppo to continue the journey and only the stragglers were still to come. Jimmy started to dismantle the machine, but admitted not feeling up to it . . . 'Wish I was back . . .'

It must have been with a sense of *deja vu* that he listened to the broadcast of the start of the race on 31 October. It was a broadcast that included the take-off of the Vega from Mildenhall as well as the arrival of Scott and Black, the winners, in Melbourne. Most of the world went wild about the achievement of the winners, and also of the Dutch competitors, Moll and Parmentier, who were placed second in both speed and handicap events and demonstrated that a transport plane (which carried a crew of four and three passengers) could reach Australia in four days. However the *Bulletin* of 31 October struck a different note:

WAS IT WORTH WHILE?
A Roman crowd would have enjoyed the England-Australia Air Race . . . the race followed the traditions of the arena.

> Gallant young lives were risked and two, those of H.D. Gilman and J.K. Baines were lost. In the general excitement nobody troubled to send an urgent wire to the bereaved parents who learnt the news when it was broadcast. The hero-worship around the finishing line was not interrupted to pay a moment's tribute to their memory.

The article went on to mention the crash by Woods and Bennett, the seizure of the engine of the winners' machine over the Timor Sea which could have been disastrous, and the problems the Mollisons encountered because the retractable undercarriage of their plane would not drop on landing. It pointed out that 20 machines started and within 5,000 miles seven were out of the race, two competitors had been killed and two injured. Although the Leader article continued its highly critical commentary, it focused on the fact that Australia was saddled with an air service to London which was out-of-date with regard to speed (a jibe that referred to the policy of the Air Minister who was prepared to accept a nine-day journey from London to Batavia by Imperial Airways while the Dutch had been able to cut their time to seven days). Although the criticism may have been justified, it certainly dampened the euphoria surrounding the race.

For Jimmy Woods, languishing in Aleppo, there was no rejoicing. He was fretting at delays, impatient for instructions from home, and suffering from an upset stomach. One diary entry conveys something of his frustration:

> What a H. of a job trying to get people to help and understand.

By 19 November, with no instructions received about what to do with the Vega, he had almost decided to fly to London when a cable arrived telling him to ship the plane back to Fremantle. By this time both he and the plane (which had been dismantled and crated in five packages and transported on the *Zafaarar* from Alexandretta) were in Port Said. It was exactly a month after his ill-fated landing at Aleppo that Jimmy sailed for home on the *Oronsay*.

ROUTE MANAGER

I don't think any other airman could have done what he did.

Van Beekman, 1936.

When Jimmy returned to Western Australia after the disappointing outcome of his participation in The Great Air Race, his career took a new direction, though in one sense it was retravelling a familiar route. As route manager for MacRobertson Miller Airlines he was responsible for planning the operations of aircraft and pilots and liaising with agents on the route from Perth to Daly Waters. Qantas flew from Brisbane via Daly Waters and Darwin to Singapore, to connect with Imperial Airways flights to London, a service which took ten days with 28 refuelling stops. For the MMA pilots, there would sometimes be a frustrating three-day wait in Daly Waters in order to pick up the in-coming London mail for Western Australia.

The length of stay was always unpredictable since it depended upon the punctuality of the flights from Darwin. The prospect of three days in Daly Waters was something few pilots looked forward to; there was nothing to do, except lounge around and read, or drink in the hotel-cum-store-cum-post-office-cum-agency. The rooms in the hotel provided a sagging bed and a chest of drawers; there was a shower outside in the yard and the lavatory was a typical 'dunny' — a hole in the ground with a wooden box covering it — surrounded by corrugated iron and clouded with flies. A vegetable garden supplemented the hotel's basic menu — plenty of meat — with an occasional carrot or pumpkin. There were two shacks in the township, but their occupants were seldom to be seen, and the only other human beings were stockmen or station workers passing through on the little-known droving route. It was nearly always hot and steamy, and the land about the settlement was flat with only a suggestion of hills in the distance.

Because the airline's operations were quite small at first, Jimmy's role sometimes overlapped with that of Cyril Gare, the accountant. There was some attempt to keep an orderly rotation of schedules but Jimmy was invariably the emergency man, ready to stand in if a pilot was ill or had met with some minor accident. He was often called upon to carry out emergency repairs — fixing a magneto, changing a tyre, cleaning spark plugs or fitting a spare propeller. There were tasks Jimmy relished: his approach to his work was all embracing, some might have said he was 'a jack of all trades', which in fact most of the early pilots had to be. More complicated repairs were handled by Frank Colquhoun, chief engineer with the airline. Frank, coming across Jimmy about to do some impromptu work with bits and pieces from his little globite case, would chiack him,

'What's that lot of rubbish you've got there?'

The catch on the case was broken so it was held shut with a strap. It was crammed full of tools, nuts and bolts and bits of wire and string. Jimmy would look up at Frank, take his pipe out of his mouth and say firmly,

'Lad, that's helped me out on many occasions', and quietly select what he needed. Frank was well aware of Jimmy's skill at repairs having worked with him when they were both employed by WA Airways.

Jimmy also played the role of public relations man, giving statements to the press about incidents and items of interest that were encountered in the day-to-day running of the airline. Above all, he did his best to see that it was being run (in the practical sense) as economically as possible. In some ways this diversity of responsibility offered the challenge he had been seeking, though inevitably, it distanced him a little from what he enjoyed doing most — flying.

102

The company began operations on 6 October 1934, with its first passenger flight, though the inaugural airmail flight was made on 9 December. In many ways the service to Daly Waters would supersede the airmail service offered by WA Airways between Perth and Adelaide (which merely cut the time from England to Australia's eastern capitals by a few days). The North West link would reduce the overall time by almost two-thirds, even allowing for unexpected delays.

The service began with three DH84 Dragon aircraft and a staff of five pilots — Jimmy Woods, Bert Hussey (who left the company almost immediately), George McCausland, Arthur Affleck and Horry Miller. Cyril Gare, the company accountant, was also an aero club pilot, but rarely flew after taking up the job of financial manager. Dave Colquhoun was the airline's engineer at the outset, and after he left to join ANA, his brother Frank, an aircraft engineer, replaced him. Frank and Jimmy would work in close association for many years and Frank's memories of Jimmy in 1988 show the warmth with which he regarded his former colleague:

> I can remember one occasion up in Broome there was a guy (I don't know where he'd come from but he was on a push bike) and he was partly crippled ... he came over to the hangar, and he was pushing his bike. There was something wrong with it I think ... and yet he was hoping to continue down to Port Hedland ... He wasn't a young fellow either ... and he was over in the hangar talking to us and asked what would be the chance of getting a ride down to Hedland on the aeroplane. 'Well', I said, 'I don't know'. Anyhow, when Jamie came out I mentioned it to him, and he said, 'Oh, I don't know'. But it touched him. He was reluctant to go against regulations, but finally he took him. I don't know whether Jamie paid his fare or not, but it wouldn't have surprised me a little bit if he had ... he was a great bloke that way.

These gestures endeared Jimmy to his colleagues and to ordinary members of the public who enjoyed his generosity in many small ways. They went down less well with his employers.

For Mollie, Jimmy's new job was a return to a familiar pattern, though unlike the early days of their marriage when she used to see him only once a week, he was based at home, but could be called

103

away at very short notice — sometimes for a few days, sometimes for weeks on end. The George Hotel that had been their home for so long changed hands in 1935. When the new management was not prepared to house Paddy, they moved to the Criterion Hotel, where there was room for both the dog and their Buick motor car. There were times too when they moved into friends' homes while the owners were overseas.

In spite of Jimmy's absences, Mollie was never lonely. She was popular, with a busy social life and was also often away, travelling to Melbourne to visit friends.

In March 1935, Arthur Affleck, flying a Dragon (VH-URW), had a mishap on landing at the 9-mile aerodrome near Wyndham. Jimmy who had just taken up his new position, had to go up to report on the damage and make an examination of the ground, already the subject of some concern. A task which he thought might take a few days developed into a lengthy repair operation which kept him away from home for many weeks.

According to the MMA agent in Wyndham the ground was

> ... covered with long grass too green to burn, many anthills visible on clear ground, probably more hidden by grass.
> Considerably washed out along the old roadway.

Jimmy found the nose of the aircraft crumpled, the front upper starboard wing broken, the outer strut port wing bent and one spar bruised. Before any repairs could be attempted the aeroplane had to be hauled back on its wheels, a complicated operation using ropes and vehicles.

Apart from repairs to the spar and wings, the nose had to be rebuilt. The Chinese storekeeper in Wyndham had an assortment of tea chests and it was with the plywood from one of these that Jimmy reconstructed the damaged nose. The plane looked a little unusual but it was able to be flown. It was towed to the take-off area, a hard-bedded track away from the treacherous, soft ground that had caused the mishap, and flown back to base.

Jimmy thoroughly enjoyed this kind of task. He never seemed to begrudge the time it took and the fact that he was away from home for weeks. 'It was his job', said Mollie. Some who worked with him thought at times that he would choose to undertake work far beyond what was asked of him. But this was not in the sense of

Affleck's crash at Wyndham, 1935.

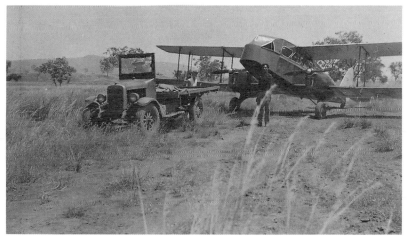

Jimmy's repair job complete.

being a martyr but because he couldn't help becoming totally involved. Possibly he also felt that no one would be able to do the job as well as he could. His own justification was that he could be more easily spared to go off for extended periods because he had no family commitments.

In October 1936, two Dutchmen, Rous and Van Beekman, flew off course on the way to Kalgoorlie and made a forced landing 100 miles south-east of the town in barren, uninhabited country. They were running short of fuel and had decided to make a landing near a salt lake, hoping that a search party would be sent out to find them. After two days with no sign of rescue, in a last desperate bid to save their lives they used the remaining three gallons of petrol to try to find some sign of habitation. After they had been flying for 25 minutes the fuel gave out and they were forced to land, once again beside a salt lake. This time searchers located their position and dropped packages of food and water. But it was Jimmy who finally brought them fuel to get airborne again. Because he was uncertain of the nature of the ground near the salt lake Jimmy tested it briefly with one wheel and then the other without actually landing. The wheel marks gave a good indication of how hard the surface was. He repeated this exercise patiently until certain the plane would be able to land — and take-off — safely. In a subsequent interview, Van Beekman said:

> That terrible bush. No life, no footprints, no game to shoot.
> We dug two holes for water but found only salt.
>   . . . All we wanted was water . . .
>   . . . I don't think any other airman could have done what he [Jimmy Woods] did. He is a marvellous pilot.

Small planes suited Jimmy. He and his machine were almost one. He understood what any aircraft was capable of and of what he was capable of in it. The complications of instrumentation threatened this relationship. Earth, sky, man, machine — these components, although at times unpredictable, had a completeness that sophisticated instrumentation challenged. Jimmy could only trust his own judgment. He knew what he could do under the most dangerous of conditions and did not believe that instruments had the same kind of reliability.

Possibly the first indication that this attitude to instruments might become a major problem occurred not so very long after Jimmy's stunning demonstration of his capabilities when rescuing Rous and Van Beekman.

In 1938 Horry Miller acquired two Lockheed 10A Electras for MMA. They were the first of the MMA fleet to have an electrically operated retractable undercarriage. They also had a new and more sophisticated radio system. The planes arrived by ship and were assembled and tested in Adelaide at Parafield.

Jimmy had to undergo familiarisation of the Lockheed before he could get endorsement on his licence for this type of aircraft. Then, after flying the first aircraft to Perth, he returned to Parafield to ferry the second plane. He prepared to take-off with First Officer Colin Brown. Horry Miller watched the machine with pride from his position near the hangars.

It was unfortunate that the crew had two subsidiary motors to contend with for the first time. While Brown was testing the radio, Jimmy, hearing its motor, mistook it for the undercarriage motor and selected that to the 'up' position. Horry looked on aghast as the undercarriage retracted with a thump and the aircraft hit the ground bending back both propellors and damaging the landing gear. The damage was repairable, but it delayed the Lockheed's departure considerably.

In the notes for his book *Early Birds*, Sir Horry Miller declared that the incident was something he accepted without rancour, if with great regret. Some colleagues however, believed that he had never really forgiven Jimmy for the crash of the Vega at Aleppo, and this second incident was neither forgiven nor forgotten.

In May of the same year, the Dunbar Hooper, as the DH83 Fox Moth ambulance plane based in Wyndham was called, was forced to land near Victoria Downs Station and an extensive air search was soon under way. The country around the station was rugged and there were fears for the safety of the plane's two occupants. Two mail planes, Murchison and Gascoyne, went out from Broome to help in the aerial search. Dr Clyde Fenton, the Northern Territory Flying Doctor, also conducted a wide-ranging search and MMA sent Jimmy Woods off in a replacement ambulance plane to assist.

It was Jim Branch, flying the Murchison, who sighted the abandoned plane. Its occupants had walked through rough

107

country to the Victoria River Depot where there was a police station and a small settlement. From there they were taken by Dr Fenton to the Victoria River Station and eventually flown back to Wyndham.

At this point Jimmy's direct involvement really began. The Dunbar Hooper had damaged a wheel on landing, so he fitted a wheel from the relief plane as a temporary measure and flew it to the station. He stayed on waiting for spare parts to arrive so that he could get the aircraft airborne again, and it was some weeks before he was able to fly it back to Perth for a complete overhaul.

It seems surprising that the company's operations manager could be missing for weeks at a time patching up planes. Of course, with the limited size of the company, all senior executives had to undertake multiple functions; because Jimmy was not tied to a regular schedule, he was the logical person to carry out these tasks. But there was probably more to it than that — something inherent in Jimmy's personality led him always to a 'hands on' approach to flying with far more emphasis on its practice than its policies. While he was obviously at ease with people in management and mixed with them socially, in practice he was happier in the role of employee, implementing the major decisions made by others. When it came to carrying out these policy decisions he enjoyed taking charge of detail and did it well. In this sense his specific skills were indispensible; few other pilots with the company at that time had the range of mechanical expertise, patience and tenacity to do what he did.

In February 1939, MMA sold a plane it had no further use for, a DH86 (VH-USD), the RMA *Brisbane,* to Tata Brothers of Bombay (Tata Brothers would later expand to become Air India), and Jimmy undertook to deliver the aircraft, flying it from Perth to Darwin and then across the Timor Sea to South-East Asia and Bombay. Clive Foreman flew with him as first officer, but was so ill as a result of vaccinations that he was unable to take over the controls at all. Mollie went along too, as a passenger, and this time it was she who kept the diary, a record with far more personal detail than Jimmy would ever have included.

On the way to Darwin, Mollie joined Jimmy in the cockpit and made notes about the weather and details of overnight stops. Bad weather had left the Broome landing strip soggy, and the plane, loaded with spare parts and extra fuel, had difficulty getting off. While they were attempting to take off Mollie was writing it all down:

> Jamie not pleased about take-off, ground very heavy — will make another attempt — this time nearly fatal — heard a bang and to my horror I can see a piece of tree on the starboard motor. One engine failed so will have to limp along to Noonkambah Station. 8am. About to land. — Wasted four hours here repairing motor . . . in the air at 12 noon heading for Wyndham.

After an overnight stop at Darwin they were ready to tackle the sea crossing — 560 miles across the Timor Sea.

> 100 miles out and about to go through a dense storm. Feel a bit nervous. Absolutely black and Jim trying to keep his eye on the water [we are] only a few hundred feet up . . . too much water for my liking.

Years later Mollie recalled further details of that crossing:

> It was the first time I think I've ever been scared because it was black and I kept thinking we were flying into the sea because we were flying so low to get away from it [the storm] . . . It just came down in torrents and when we landed there wasn't a bit of silver paint on that plane. The rain had knocked the whole lot off, it was so heavy.

After stopping briefly at Koepang they flew on and landed later the same day at Rambang to refuel. The place had been a refuelling stop for Imperial Airways, but there was no telephone at the airstrip so it was some time before the petrol arrived on a wagon. As it appeared, local inhabitants streamed towards the fuel drums and while the petrol was transferred to the plane, clustered around trying to catch the drips. Clive Foreman was asleep under the wing, still groggy from his vaccinations, and Jimmy, busy with the refuelling, warned Mollie not to let anyone aboard, fearing they might run amok. Eventually they took off for Bali where they spent the night. The rest of the trip passed uneventfully and they delivered the plane in Bombay.

It was now five years since Jimmy had joined MMA and whether the job measured up to his expectations it is hard to say. It is unlikely that he had ever had a long term vision of his future with the company, because he always tended to live from day to day; to cope with situations as they arose. There had been moments of excitement and danger, but there had been nothing to match the personal challenge of his solo flight in 1933 or the Great Air Race of 1934. He was already 46: middle-aged. Mollie was still in her early thirties and for much of their married life they had been apart, yet neither was anxious to 'settle down' in the accepted sense. Jimmy was not an acquisitive man: his only valuable possession was his motor car, a Buick, which over the years he had updated and cared for meticulously. Whether it was Mollie's idea or something they decided together, they moved in 1939 to a newly-built block of flats, Abordale, at the upper end of St George's Terrace. Although rented, it was their first real 'home'. There was garage space for the Buick and room for Paddy.

With Jimmy's ample salary (he was paid twice the amount Horry paid himself) they could look forward to a more settled and very comfortable life. Whether this was really what Jimmy wanted is doubtful. He seemed to need an 'edge' of risk, though at this time Australia's entry into the Second World War meant that life once more had become unpredictable. Some of the MMA fleet was requisitioned for use by the RAAF and a number of its employees released for war service; some including Jimmy Woods and Frank Colquhoun, were 'man-powered' and compulsorily exempted from active service.

It was not until Japan entered the war that the role of MMA changed in some respects and there were new opportunities to test Jimmy's particular skills.

THE HOME FRONT: DONKEY POWER

> There was no other pilot except perhaps Alec Whitham who
> had the skill and temperament to undertake such a task.
>
> Frank Colquhoun

With his usual determination, Jimmy decided that, in spite of
being officially man-powered, he would still try to get entry into
the RAAF. At his age, it was unlikely that he would be accepted for
active service, but this didn't deter him at all.

The Wing-Commander at Pearce Air Force base near Perth was
a personal friend and Jimmy talked to him about the possibility of
getting into the flying boat squadron. He managed to get written
recommendation to the Secretary of the Air Board for a com-
paratively senior rank but nothing came of it.

The following September Jimmy submitted another application which he endorsed *Flying Boats Only*. Because the first
application had suggested some doubt about his release from
essential civilian work, the application was given a further
endorsement by the Air Board: *Hold until Applicant Advises his
Position*. Almost a year later, possibly as a result of the Battle of
Britain, Jimmy sent off another letter, this time to the Minister for
Air, John McEwen, asking for an appropriate appointment in the
RAAF. He stipulated that he wanted to join the Sunderland
Flying Boat Squadron and that he hoped for a rank not less than

Squadron Leader. The Minister replied that appointments were not made on the basis of applicants' conditions, but that if Woods were to submit an unconditional application it would receive 'the fullest consideration and a prompt decision'.

Jimmy was accepted by the RAAF but not in the way that he had hoped — all civilians with skills that could be of use in the event of a direct attack on Australia and invasion were incorporated into the reserve forces of the three services; on 1 January 1944, James Wood was appointed to the RAAF Reserves as Squadron Leader. His appointment was terminated on 30 September 1959.

If Jimmy was disappointed that he couldn't play a more active role in the war, Mollie was relieved. Fatalistic about decisions beyond her control, she believed that it was meant for the best. The roles Jimmy was shortly to play in one of the most remarkable salvage operations in Australia seemed to confirm this belief.

On 7 December 1941, the Japanese bombed Pearl Harbour and the war in the Pacific began. In little over two months the Japanese had occupied Guam and Wake Islands; Hong Kong had surrendered and they had landed in the Philippines and the Dutch East Indies. On February 15 1942 they invaded Singapore.

On the same day a Lockheed 10A Electra took off from Darwin bound for Perth. On board were several passengers who had escaped from Singapore, including a Mrs Hagemeijer and her two sons, Allen, aged four and Alexander aged two and a half. They were travelling under false passports. The children's father, a maritime agent in Singapore, had arranged this because his connections with wealthy Chinese businessmen meant that if caught by the Japanese, the whole family would be executed.

Jim Branch piloted the Lockheed and Reg Bagwell was co-pilot. They landed safely at Wyndham and took off for Derby at 2.40pm.

Ninety minutes out from Wyndham the starboard engine failed. The aircraft began to vibrate and to lose height. Captain Branch managed to ease it over the King Leopold and Napier ranges, searching all the time for a possible landing site. Eventually the plane belly-landed in a black soil bog.

For the passengers it was a traumatic experience. Mrs Metherell writing to her husband, said:

> ... the vibration in the plane was simply awful. I ... thought the plane would break up in mid-air and all the time we were losing height ... we managed to hop across a range of hills, and ... the pilot landed with the wheels up ... we were thrown violently forward and [the plane] made an awful tearing noise... the first officer looking very wild-eyed dashed past us shouting to keep your seats [he ran down the aisle to open the passenger door at the rear of the aircraft]. All this time I was trying to open the belt because I thought the plane might catch fire.

Allen Metherell, later in life, recalled the total silence of the passengers; the terror on one woman's face; the gasps and thuds as the plane crashed and the clatter of his mother's handbag as it burst open scattering its contents.

This was only the beginning of their ordeal.

Mrs Metherell also had vivid memories:

> ... we found ourselves floundering around in thick black mud, and wherever we looked we could see thick black mud, pampas grass and trees (at least half-dead and of stunted growth) in the distance.

The humidity was unbearable and at dusk the mosquitoes came in swarms. The only light was from Reg Bagwell's battery-operated torch, and emergency rations were meagre. The passengers were hot, hungry and frightened. In the darkness they returned to the aircraft to escape the mosquitoes and to try to sleep. It was a long night.

The aircraft's radio was still working and their plight was soon made known, but it was late the following afternoon before help of any sort materialised. Jimmy Woods, who was flying from Derby to Wyndham in MMA's only other Lockheed, had been instructed to locate the crashed plane and drop some supplies. In spite of a painstaking search he could not find the plane. When it crashed it had become embedded in the boggy soil; this and the grassy nature of the country successfully camouflaged it. Although Jim Branch and Reg Bagwell could not see the search plane, they could hear the drone of its engines and so started a fire. Eventually, spotting the smoke, Jimmy flew towards the camp site, coming in low to drop the first of the relief supplies. Out tumbled the bundles, one after another. The passengers' fears were lessened slightly. They had been located and the supplies, though basic, eased their hunger.

While Jimmy was carrying out the immediate relief plan, at the MMA office in Perth the long-term rescue was discussed. There were two things to be done: passengers and crew had to be got out, and the plane had to be salvaged. The company could not afford to lose an aircraft, so no matter how impossible the task seemed that plane had to be repaired, got out of the swamp and back into the air.

It was decided that the chief engineer, Frank Colquhoun, should fly to Derby, then go by vehicle to Meda Station, some 30 miles from the crash site and in phone contact with Derby. From there he would take a ground party to the plane, assess the situation and work out a plan.

While these official plans were being discussed, an unofficial rescue operation was underway, organised by Ned Delower, manager of Napier Downs Station. Jimmy had advised Ned about the crashed plane by message drop but had been unable to give precise details of its location. Ned gathered such equipment as he considered essential and set off with four aboriginal stockmen and ten horses. For two days they scoured the bush unsuccessfully.

'Those men of mine could have tracked you to the gates of Hell on the ground, but aeroplanes don't leave tracks in the sky', he was to recall.

Then, when they were about to give up, they caught sight of a small plane circling and diving about five miles to the west. They rode off in that direction for about an hour, then Ned fired three shots into the air. Five minute's later a cloud of smoke rose from the bush and shortly after they rode into the camp.

Ned rounded up some roaming cattle, shot and butchered one of them and prepared a meal of steak and potatoes, tinned fruit (from the air drop), bread, butter and jam. Years later, Allen Metherell remembered that, as a four-year-old, he thought it was the best meal he had ever eaten. The morale of the stranded passengers was lifted immediately.

Then the official search party from Meda Station arrived, led by Frank Colquhoun, who assessed the situation and decided that the first priority was to fly the passengers out. To do this it was necessary to find a patch of ground dry and flat enough for a small aircraft to land and take-off. They eventually found a spot, about half a mile from the crash site across a creek. It was shaped like an hour glass, with a billabong at each end and two other ponds in the middle about 30 yards apart. It seemed possible, so Frank thought, that if a pilot came in with the lowest possible approach and touched down right at the edge of the billabong, he would be able to get his run through, but it would be hazardous. Taking off would be even more hazardous. There was no doubt in Frank's mind that Jimmy was the pilot for the job:

> There was no other pilot except perhaps Alec Whitham who had the skill and temperament to undertake such a task.

Jimmy knew the North West intimately and understood the weather conditions. His particular skill was taking off and landing with minimum length. While he never took unnecessary risks, he was always prepared to have a go at the most difficult tasks.

Before Jimmy could make the landing they had to prepare the strip. All day they toiled, assisted by Ned Delower and the stockmen. Boulders had to be rolled out of the way, smaller rocks cleared, bushes uprooted, trees lopped and roots grubbed out. They returned to camp late in the afternoon, grimy and sweat-stained, and cleaned up in one of the pools which they dubbed their 'bogey hole'.

A week after the crash the strip was ready and Reg Bagwell got in radio contact with Derby. At about noon a faint hum could be heard. The group on the ground watched as a far-off dot in the sky grew larger. As it came in low to assess the strip, the marking on its side, VH-UZU, stood out clearly. Jimmy Woods, as Frank had predicted, was flying the plane. He made a couple of sweeps of the landing site, then came in as low as possible and put the plane down exactly as planned. He climbed from the cockpit, quite unperturbed, his hat on his head and his pipe in his mouth.

'Hullo lads', he said, and accepted their offer of a mug of tea.

It was already the afternoon and the evacuation of passengers had to be undertaken as quickly as possible. With the first person aboard, Jimmy prepared for take-off while those on the ground watched anxiously. Everything went according to plan.

The Cessna ran down the strip, rose steeply, cleared the trees and flew off — a rapidly disappearing speck — in the direction of Derby. Soon it was back and the process was repeated with a second passenger.

When Jimmy landed for the third time it was about 6pm and the Metherells were still to be evacuated. With only one passenger seat Jimmy was unwilling to overload the aircraft, but Mrs Metherell, understandably, would not allow her family to be separated. Finally Jimmy agreed that they should fly together and after a successful take-off they were on their way to Derby.

This was one of the few occasions when Jimmy's normally placid nature was tested. Both he and Mrs Metherell had been under considerable strain. The younger child had contracted Dengue Fever and became distressed during the night. Jimmy, in addition to having given up his mosquito-proofed room to the family, was kept awake by the continuous screams. Unaware of the child's condition he made it clear that he thought the boy was thoroughly spoilt. He and Mrs Metherell exchanged a few terse words. Jimmy was normally very tolerant of children and his reaction at this time was quite uncharacteristic.

With the passengers safely out of the way and Jim Branch flown out to resume regular duties, Frank Colquhoun and his team were able to turn their attention to the damaged aircraft. Their first task was to jack it up out of the mud and release the wheels. Then they could dismantle the damaged engine, replace it and carry out maintenance work on the new engine.

They had little equipment other than that brought out by the Napier Downs and Meda parties. Other equipment and parts had to be flown to Derby and either dropped by parachute or brought in by the Cessna. They had already built a support for the plane from logs, criss-crossing them and packing them under a wing. Gradually, with the aid of additional equipment, they jacked the plane out of the mud and were able to lower the wheels. It was hot dirty work — they were burnt black by the sun, bitten by marsh flies, and ached with rheumatics caused by sleeping on the damp ground. When Jimmy flew them out a roll of hessian they were able to make some stretchers, using forked timber which at least got them up off the ground and gradually the stiffness in their joints improved.

Salvaging the Electra, Napier Downs, February, 1942.

Sometimes, because of the weather conditions, Jimmy was unable to land. If he was ferrying food supplies — canned meat, bread, flour or potatoes — he could risk dropping them. Mostly they were packed in a cornsack padded with straw, and as he flew in low he would pitch out the sack when he thought it would hit the right spot. Almost invariably, as it hit the ground, the sack would split and the contents would finish up in a billabong. The bread would be soaked and soon became mouldy.

Before returning to their properties, the station people helped remove the propellers and manhandle the failed engine from the mounting. Ned Delower agreed to return later to help shift the repaired aircraft to the landing strip.

During the next few weeks Jimmy made something like 30 flights between Derby and the site, frequently flying in difficult conditions, uncertain whether he would be able to land, especially if there was a strong cross-wind. Sometimes he landed but was unable to take-off again because of cloud or changed wind conditions. In these circumstances he was forced to stay overnight and wasn't very impressed with what he called the 'air-conditioned' quarters.

After the replacement engine had been fitted, the aircraft had to be moved to the landing strip where final maintenance and repairs could be completed. This meant shifting a three-ton machine out of a swamp and across a creek. They planned to use donkey-power.

Three crossings were built over the creek for each of the plane's wheels using the stockpile of logs. Ned Delower was notified by message drop that they were ready for him and he spent the next day or so rounding up as many donkeys as he could from the ranges around the station. These donkeys had been used to the freedom of the range and had not been worked for a long time — probably some had never worked — and they didn't respond very well to being rounded up. Eventually Ned had a team of 30 or so and set off with his stockmen.

Nothing seemed to go entirely to plan. The night after the crossings were completed there was a severe storm up country. The creek flooded and washed out their crossing. Frank Colquhoun recalled:

> It took our camp gear and stuff and we had to go and search for this next morning down the creek . . . we had to build the crossing again . . . Ned Delower arrived with his donkeys before we got those crossings built up again. Then we were ready to haul the aeroplane out.

They managed to face the plane in the general direction they wanted it to go, then cut down a large kurrajong log which they laid in front of the aircraft, with chains between the axle and the log to attach the harness for the donkeys.

The donkeys didn't want to be harnessed. They were fidgety and the ground was very wet and muddy. As they stamped about their small hooves soon churned up the mud.

'I didn't know anything about donkeys except that they were four-legged animals', said Frank Colquhoun. 'We learnt a lot about donkeys in that first attempt . . . we reckoned on about ten rows of three, but in the process of getting them lined up and into the harness the ground got so boggy, some of the donkeys finished up to their bellies in mud, and so hopelessly bogged they were useless.'

They decided to reduce the number of donkeys to seven rows of four and to approach from a different angle. Once they were

Shifting the Electra to firmer ground, Napier Downs.

harnessed again Frank discovered:

> With donkeys it's either go or stop. There's no in between . . .
> to get them to go, that was the thing, and to keep them
> moving. Some of the donkeys were extra reluctant. Now, Ned
> Delower, he had all the tricks in the world, from twisting
> their tails to get them to move, to lifting up and splashing
> water in their ears. It was no good hitting them. It was like
> hitting a bag of wheat.

Jimmy lent a hand too; prodding the donkeys, helping to head
them in the right direction.

At last the animals began to move, and the donkey team took up
the slack of the chains. Gradually the aeroplane's wheels started to
turn. Round they went, moving forward about eight feet. Then
they stopped turning, gummed up with sticky black mud and
bound by wiry grass. But the donkeys didn't stop pulling and the
plane's wheels scored two deep trenches as the machine was
dragged towards the creek. Half-way across the creek the logs on
one of the temporary crossings shifted and the wheel thumped
down into the creek.

Ned Delower cursed.

The donkeys were unhitched, the plane jacked up and the crossing rebuilt. It was a slow process but eventually the operation was completed and the Lockheed was across the creek, ready for final repairs. Ned and his donkeys went back to Napier Downs and Jimmy flew back to Derby.

It took the engineers the best part of another week to put finishing touches to the replacement engine, carry out some check runs, repair wing flaps and clean up the other engine, picking out the dried mud and grass from around the cylinders.

It was important that the strip should be as dry as possible for take-off. Any surface water that had fallen during the night had to be mopped up, using old pieces of rag and hessian. They also splashed excess fuel over the strip and set it alight to help dry and harden the surface. Then they radioed for Jimmy.

As he landed there was a slight cross-wind coming in at an angle.

'I think it's our chance', said Frank. 'What about it Jim?'

'Well, lad', said Jimmy. 'I don't know. Let's walk up and down and have a look.'

They covered the length of the strip, testing for soft spots. Finally Jimmy took his pipe out of his mouth and said,

'All right. Righto! Righto lad. We'll give it a go.'

Jimmy started the engine and Frank walked down the strip in front of the plane to guide it through the difficult spots. At the far end of the runway Jimmy turned the plane and the inside wheel went down a hole. Everyone on site pushed and shoved and lifted; with full engine power they were able to pull the wheel out and straighten the plane just at the edge of the billabong.

Frank climbed aboard. He was to accompany Jimmy and, provided all went well, Reg Bagwell would take the others out in the Cessna the following day.

The Lockheed was a much bigger plane than the Cessna and the makeshift strip left no margin for delay in getting airborne, yet Frank had no doubt that Jimmy could do it. As the engines gathered speed the men on the ground watched silently. Would it lift off as expected? Would it clear the trees?

As it rose in the air and flew off towards Derby there was a sense of utter relief. Their team effort had worked. No lives had been lost and the plane was airworthy again. In terms of man-hours it had been a costly exercise, but labour was available; replacement aeroplanes in wartime were not.

FRONT LINE

From his action I knew I dealt with a very thorough and
unswerving character.

Flying Officer Petschi

In February 1942 the unthinkable happened and Australia was
subjected to direct enemy attack. Japanese forces had swept
beyond Singapore and were threatening the Dutch East Indies.
Then on 19 February, Darwin was bombed. Never again would
Australians see themselves as inviolate.

Refugees had been pouring into Australia, at first from
Singapore and then from the East Indies, as Dutch nationals,
especially women and children, were evacuated as speedily as
possible. They were crammed into flying boats bound for Darwin,
then after its bombing, to Broome, where Roebuck Bay was
suitable for the landing of flying boats. Not only were civiliams
being evacuated; there were also American service personnel from
the Philippines. It was a frenetic time.

Darwin had for some time been a possible target for enemy
attack but Wyndham and Broome were regarded as less vulnerable.
Then, with the upgrading of Broome airport when it became a
refuelling station for the RAAF, it too became a potential target.

Broome was not really equipped to cope with the influx of
people who were arriving daily to wait overnight for flights to

Perth or Sydney. With the exception of one woman, Miss Bardwell, who stayed behind to attend to the telephone exchange, all local women and children had been evacuated south. Hotel and private accommodation were stretched to the limit, though many evacuees elected to stay aboard the flying boats anchored in the bay, rather than go ashore to take a chance on what accommodation was available. There were several reasons for this decision — perhaps the most significant was the 24-foot tide. Passengers who wished to go ashore at low tide had to squelch through soft mud to the jetty, climb it, then walk a further half mile or so to shore. The elderly, and those with young children, preferred to stay aboard their aircraft overnight.

On the morning of 3 March there were 16 flying boats on Roebuck Bay with many women and children aboard. The tide was in. On Broome airstrip there were a further seven aircraft — large bombers and transport planes. There had been reports of a Japanese reconnaissance plane doing some investigative sweeps the afternoon before, and a plane had been heard overhead just before dawn. Later, some residents recalled having seen flashing lights signalling from the jetty at the time the plane was heard, but no one anticipated the subsequent events.

In between ferrying supplies to the party working on the stranded Lockheed Electra at Napier Downs, Jimmy Wood was flying the mail run between Port Hedland and Darwin. On the morning of 3 March he was about to take off from Wyndham, bound for Derby. The Electra was at weight limit, loaded with spare parts: it was touch and go whether it would get off at all. Then, as the plane began to lift, a Dragon swept right in its path. The incident happened so fast that the plane was away almost before Jimmy and MMA's Broome-based mechanic, John Fisher, had time to react; in any case, keeping that Electra in the air was more important than speculating on a near miss, and Jimmy was doing all he could to get height.

Once at a safe cruising height they set course for Derby where they learned that they had just missed being caught up in a Japanese raid on Wyndham. The Dragon that had startled them had been taking evasive action to escape a Japanese plane. No one could understand how the Electra, lumbering along the airstrip, had escaped unscathed. The only explanation seemed to be that the dust it had stirred up from the unsealed earth strip had successfully camouflaged it.

At the same time as the Wyndham air raid, Broome was also attacked. Japanese Zeros, fitted with extra fuel tanks to extend their range, had ditched the tanks after using the reserve fuel and flown on towards Broome, confident that they could sustain a lengthy raid and make it back to Koepang. Shortly after 7am they attacked the bombers and transport planes on the Broome airstrip, leaving the ground littered with burnt-out and burning hulks of planes. One of the US Liberator bombers had managed to take-off but was brought down by enemy fire; although two men escaped from the plane after it crashed into the sea, both subsequently died.

There was no deliberate attack on the township, but the aerodrome was so close and the town so small, that inhabitants assumed they were also the target. Some attempt was made by civil defence forces to offer resistance and at least one enemy plane was brought down. At the same time, other Japanese fighter planes attacked the flying boats lying in Roebuck Bay — ideal targets for their fire, and giving no hint they were bulging with civilian occupants who had slept aboard overnight.

The Japanese pilots wheeled their Zeros and flew in screaming dives towards the anchored aircraft. Within seconds machine-gun fire and bombs struck planes; many burst into flames as fuel from punctured petrol tanks poured into the water and was ignited.

Those women who managed to escape the blazing shells of planes leapt into the water, many clasping children. Some were burnt to death, others drowned and some were presumably taken by sharks. There were few survivors. Thirteen bodies of civilian women and children were later recovered and identified, and the bodies of a number of unidentified persons were also found.

After half an hour of unrelenting attack the Zeros zoomed out of their final dives and flew back to Koepang. Smoke and silence blanketed the bay and town. As Jimmy flew in to land on the Broome airstrip he was appalled by the sight. Smoke rose in clouds and blackened fuselages made landing hazardous. With such an obstacle course to negotiate it was almost inevitable that he should blunder against one of the wrecked American planes. The fuselage and wings of his Electra were undamaged, but one propeller was slightly bent and gouged. It would be impossible to get the plane

124

airborne in such a condition yet it was imperative that it be available to evacuate survivors. This was the kind of situation that tested Jimmy's ingenuity and, as often in the past, the simplest course, while drastic, was the one he opted for.

To straighten the propeller tip he would require tools and equipment and there was nothing really serviceable on that devastated strip. To go into town would take valuable time, and it was essential to get people out as soon as possible in case of a repeat raid. Without hesitation, Jimmy made the decision to cut the bent, gouged section of the blade tip off, and crop the sound blade to match. This was necessary if the blades were to balance and the engine function well enough to get airborne. It was the kind of spontaneous action that earned the respect and admiration of his more cautious colleagues, though it didn't please Horry Miller.

As soon as the emergency repair job was done, Jimmy crammed as many survivors as possible aboard and flew south to Port Hedland. He made several such flights, on one occasion squeezing 22 persons into his 10-seater aircraft.

Returning from one of these flights Jimmy sighted an aircraft stranded on the Ninety Mile Beach, 100 miles south of Broome. It was a Royal Netherlands Navy seaplane that had been forced down through lack of fuel, though Jimmy was not to know this at the time. In a report of the incident, the pilot, Flying Officer Petschi, said that he had been ordered to take the X-36 to Broome but was forced down because northerly winds had meant an abnormal use of petrol. He anchored off-shore and sent a message to his group commander at Broome, expecting him to send petrol.

Less than an hour later another Royal Netherlands Navy plane flew over at a very low altitude but failed to see the X-36. Shortly after a KNILM plane did sight it and Petschi fired off a red flare. The plane circled and dropped a message which fell into the sea and was lost, although the pilot signalled that he understood the problem before flying off to the north. Two more planes passed over — a US Lockheed P-38 and a Qantas flying boat — but neither paid any attention to the stranded plane.

Petschi assumed that because the planes were hugging the coast and flying very low, there was Japanese air activity in the area. To avoid inviting attack he weighed anchor and let the wind push the plane onto the beach. As soon as it ran aground, he sent the

125

passengers (all women and children) with an officer to take shelter in the dunes out of sight as far as possible; then, with the rest of the crew, he secured the plane. It was soon after this that Jimmy Woods flew overhead. Petschi fired another red flare and Jimmy came down low and circled above him. Within minutes a message fluttered down. Jimmy had seized an air-sickness bag and scrawled the following message:

> Answer me the following questions by radio in the 45 metre band with 'yes' or 'no'. Don't betray position.
> 1. Engine trouble?
> 2. Wounded?
> 3. Shot down?
> 4. Enough petrol?
> 5. Can you start again?
>
> At Broome all flying boats and land planes have been destroyed during an air raid. I will ask for help and petrol immediately in Broome or Port Hedland.

The paper bag had a white cloth attached to it and landed about 30 feet from the plane.

Petschi replied immediately explaining that their water supply was very low. In his later report he recorded:

> From his action I knew I dealt with a thorough and unswerving character.

Jimmy Woods continued his flight to Broome, reported on the X-36 and loaded more survivors onto his plane. On his way south again he left a message at a cattle station located fairly close to the stranded plane, asking that a rescue party be sent out by car. He then dropped another message to the Dutch group explaining that help would be coming and that petrol was already on its way.

The following morning the marooned party ran out of water. No rescue team had appeared and a land search by the Dutch crew members failed to find either water or habitation and their position looked desperate. Mosquitoes had made life hell during the night and the passengers were almost at the end of their tether. The sight of Woods' plane brought relief and Petschi fired a white distress flare. When the Electra flew off without any reciprocal signal the group despaired of rescue. But their fears were groundless. Jimmy had flown straight to the cattle station, landed and asked why the group had not been picked up. He was told that in spite of searching all night they had failed to locate either the plane or its occupants.

There was something of a 'Biggles' about Jimmy in this kind of situation. Although his actions were probably quite spontaneous, subconsciously he seemed to be playing a role of 'rescuer'. There was a certain quality of game playing, of 'getting it right', of following a 'procedure'. In this sense he was quite meticulous about procedure (witness his note), yet it was the very thing about officialdom that drove him mad. When he set up his own rules, he followed them impeccably, but as far as others' rules were concerned he was mostly non-conforming.

On this particular morning, he took a Mr Gudjerry from the cattle station aboard the Electra and flew him over the stranded plane to pin-point its position, also taking along several desperately needed items. As the Electra flew low over the group, Jimmy flung out a rolled up magazine on which he had marked the position of a windmill. When Petschi sent one of his men out with a kettle to show that the message had been understood, Jimmy dived towards the man and flew in the direction of the windmill, circling it to make sure its position was quite clear. Then, as slowly as possible, he flew towards the dunes and threw out a drum of water which, not unexpectedly, broke upon impact. Jimmy then flung several wrapped bottles of water (which remained intact), a bottle of milk for the children, a bag of bread, another of sugar, tea bags, tins of milk powder, corned beef and jam, tobacco, cigarette papers and matches. Finally out floated another message to say that Mr Gudjerry would be out in the evening to rescue the civilians and that the schooner *Nicholbay* was on her way with petrol: 'If the ship has not arrived by dark, make a little fire, otherwise the ship may pass by', wrote Jimmy.

Finally the group was rescued, the fuel arrived and Petschi was able to take-off. In his report of the incident Petschi detailed the part Jimmy Woods had played, and in July 1942, Jimmy received an official letter of thanks from the Senior Naval Officer of the RNN in Australia, FW Coster. In recognition of his services Queen Wilhelmina of the Netherlands bestowed the honour of Chevalier of the Order of Orange Nassau upon James Woods on

18 February 1943. Jimmy received hundreds of congratulatory telegrams, one suggesting that it was as well he wasn't an Irishman. Jimmy appeared to take all the publicity quite calmly, yet he was both delighted and moved to be recognised in this way, and kept the cuttings from newspaper reports and several copies of Flying Officer Petschi's report.

DITCHED

I thought, 'I'm going to die, and so far from home?'

Rodney Pyke

During the latter part of the War, MMA was required to cut back its operations in Western Australia and Jimmy was seconded to ANA in Melbourne to fly between that city and Sydney and Hobart. Mollie stayed in Perth doing voluntary work to help raise money for Camp Comforts. A team of women ran the Silver Bullet, a tea rooms, which for most of the war years took over the premises of the Moana Cafe in Hay Street, serving morning and afternoon teas, and lunches. Mollie's specialty was the Silver Bullet 'Special' salad, which had 'everything' in it, including olives and tuna, something quite innovative for Perth at that time, where salad usually meant shredded lettuce, sliced tomato, flute-edged cucumber and beetroot that bled over every other ingredient.

Later, after a short time in hospital to have her appendix removed, Mollie continued her voluntary work. She would turn her hand to baking hundreds of scones each morning, and in the evenings joined others as dancing partners for servicemen at the YMCA, later taking a turn at the sink washing up the supper dishes.

With the war in Europe over and the conflict with Japan in its final stages, the RAAF was prepared to replace the two DH86 aircraft it had requisitioned from MMA, and Jimmy Woods who was back in Perth by this time, was sent with Frank Colquhoun to Amberley Air Force base in Queensland to repair the planes (if necessary) and fly them back to Western Australia. The first of the two planes was in good condition and Jimmy was able to ferry it home straight away. The other was in pieces.

While Jimmy flew the first home, Frank and Charlie Rolandi (who had flown over from WA to join them), set to work gathering up the parts of the plane which were located all over the depot. The fuselage was in one place, the wings in another, the propellers were somewhere else and smaller items of hardware were mixed up with spare parts from other aircraft. They managed to locate most of the parts and get them together in a hangar. Replacements for parts that were still missing they were able to beg from either Qantas or ANA.

Over a period of seven or eight weeks they assembled and repaired the aircraft, though there were several small items still missing. Always resourceful, they made do with ordinary aircraft bolts or hardware — it was necessary only to make the aircraft sufficiently airworthy to be flown back to Perth where it could be stripped down and completely overhauled. When they considered the plane ready, Jimmy was sent for and test flew it.

The plane's brakes were found to be ineffective. With the DH86 it was important that the brakes worked well because the aircraft had a habit of 'ground looping'. A ground loop could occur towards the end of a landing run, when the aircraft, though well and truly on the ground, would suddenly swing sideways and do a complete loop, often causing the landing gear to collapse although the plane itself did not overturn. If this swing happened early in the run, the landing gear could be side-swiped off and crushed. Frank Colquhoun, in retrospect, said of the DH86:

> It [ground looping] was a well-known trait. Everyone had trouble with the early DH86, and the pilot had to be very alert in the early run; ready for it to swing, then try to counter with full opposite braking, plus application of full outer engine power on the inside side of the swing. If applied fully at the first sign of a swing it could be an effective counter, but once a substantial swing developed, nothing could arrest a full ground loop.

With the faulty brakes, the problem of a ground loop could be doubly hard to handle.

Frank knew some of the ANA people at Archerfield airfield, not far from Amberley, and he thought that if he and Jimmy could get the plane across he would be able to persuade the United States Air Force repair team to regrind the brake drums and resurface the brake shoes. But when he and Jimmy thought about it, they realised that there were a lot of things about that aircraft that were only makeshift and that it would be wise to make the trip to Archerfield on a weekend when the Department of Civil Aviation staff would not be around. They planned to leave Amberley at midday Saturday, get the brakes fixed at Archerfield and be out of there on Sunday to head for Sydney on the first leg of their flight home.

As they landed at Archerfield the plane blew a tyre and they had to get help from ANA to repair it. This delayed them somewhat, but eventually the brakes were put in order. Then, on their landing run at Sydney airport, predictably, the landing gear went down on the left-hand side in a ground loop.

Even in those days there was a good deal of international traffic in and out of Sydney and an overseas plane was due to land 15 minutes later. A terse message came from the control tower: 'If you don't get that bloody rubbish off the strip in ten minutes, we'll bulldoze it off'.

There were some low baggage trolleys on the tarmac and, with some assistance, Frank and Jimmy dragged them across and managed to get the aeroplane up sufficiently to sit the damaged landing gear on the trolleys and push the DH86 off the strip. Eventually the plane was repaired and flown to Perth. There must have been some kind of jinx on that plane. It gave constant trouble and was the aircraft in which Jim Branch was killed at Geraldton, though on that occasion a ground loop was not the cause.

The post-war years were difficult ones for Jimmy Woods. There were increasing changes in the airline industry which he found hard to accept and adapt to. His tenacity, which had always been a strength, was increasingly seen as something of a failing — a stubborn clinging to old ways. Yet Jimmy was willing to adapt: on his own terms and in his own time.

He was 52 when the war ended — too young to retire, even if he had wanted to, not really suited by temperament or experience to become a full-time administrator tied to a desk, and increasingly out-of-step with the way in which the industry was heading. Yet he had a lifetime's experience, and skills that few young pilots, whose training had been in combat planes, would have had the opportunity or time to acquire.

MMA took on a number of such young men, who were enthusiastic and eager to learn, and they were mostly placed as first officers with experienced captains like Jimmy Woods or Alec Whitham. There was another pilot who had also been with the company for a long time, though he was a much younger man than Jimmy Woods. His name was Cyril Kleinig.

In 1939 the South Australian services provided by MMA were transferred to Guinea Airways, and Kleinig, who had been managing that branch of the company ever since Horry Miller had taken over the North West airmail route in Western Australia in 1934, was brought across to Perth as a pilot of first officer rank. He was 27 years old. Nine years earlier, as a youth, he had persuaded Horry to let him spend weekends helping in the Commercial Aviation Company's hangar at Parafield. Within months he was training to be a pilot. Horry regarded him as a protegee, and it is very likely that when he brought him to Western Australia in 1939, he had at the back of his mind the idea of Kleinig as a possible successor. It would seem that Horry's loyalties were divided. He also had strong ties and obligations to Jimmy Woods, his route manager for the past five years, yet it is unlikely that he saw any reason why the two loyalties should conflict. He and Jimmy were the same age and would probably retire at the same time. It was important that a younger man be ready to fill the gap. Had he discussed the matter with Jimmy possibly there would have been no misunderstanding and much of the bitterness of the next few years might have been avoided. But Horry was a man who worked through his own problems and solved them in his own way.

For a number of reasons Jimmy Woods and Cyril Kleinig felt a mutual antipathy from the start. Kleinig was intensely keen, hard-working and dedicated to the company, but he was not willing to accept advice. Jimmy was equally dedicated and hard-working, and although he was easy-going, he liked to do things his way. Both men were teetotal, but while Jimmy was tolerant of

132

others' drinking, Cyril was not. Their approach to flying could not have been more different either. Kleinig was a stickler for rules, Jimmy would happily flout them if he felt they did not apply to a particular situation. Another source of disagreement was their preferred method of flying when there was cloud about. Jimmy would usually choose to fly beneath the cloud where horizon and landmarks were clearly visible. This low flying meant a pretty bumpy ride and less margin for error if height was necessary to allow for corrective action of some kind. Kleinig preferred to rely on instruments and fly above the cloud where there was little or no turbulence.

Even though their personalities clashed, this in itself might not have mattered so very much, but Jimmy seemed to feel threatened by Cyril and, as route manager, made life quite hard at times for the young pilot. Jimmy may have had cause to feel slighted on occasions, too, when it became increasingly obvious that Horry Miller was more inclined to listen to Cyril, especially when matters relating to instrument flying were discussed.

Kleinig was a highly competent Instrument Rules pilot, and the newer planes were more sophisticated and relied increasingly upon instrumentation. Jimmy was not coping very well with instrument flying. It was a bit late in life for him to make the radical change from Visual Flight Rules to Instrument Flight Rules Operation and, though he undertook special training in Melbourne, he did not acquit himself very well. He would not concede that instruments could replace vision, intuition and experience. Kleinig, on the other hand, had none of the prejudices of older 'seat of the pants' pilots against instrument flying.

The next few years saw increasing friction between the two men and Kleinig may well have considered resigning. Jimmy would never have contemplated such a solution. It would have been a sign of weakness on his part and stoicism was second nature to him. He would have felt that 'what can't be cured, must be endured'.

It was obvious that sooner or later there would be a showdown of some kind between the two men, but it is unlikely that anyone could have predicted the way in which the struggle would finally be resolved.

Just before 5am on the morning of 17 June 1946, Captain James

Woods was warming up the engines of the Lockheed Electra 10A, VH-ABW, prior to taking-off from Broome for Darwin, with First Officer Rodney Pyke at the dual controls and Forrest Hamersley as supernumerary. There were five passengers onboard. It was still dark and fog of varying intensity was drifting across the airstrip. MMA's Douglas, VH-AEU, piloted by Alec Whitham, was also waiting to take-off — for Port Hedland. As that airstrip was also under fog, Whitham decided to delay departure. Jimmy should have delayed take-off too, but he had flown in and out of Broome hundreds of times, sometimes in foggy conditions. Mostly, if there were fog, it was a matter of quickly getting up a few hundred feet and one would be through it and into clear sky. On this particular morning, it seems Jimmy had no qualms whatsoever.

Rodney Pyke had recently joined MMA after service with the RAAF flying single-engined aircraft. He had never made an instrument take-off before and it was his first flight with Jimmy Woods as captain. Neither man knew much about the other's temperament or skills except from reputation and hearsay. It was customary for the captain to give the first officer the opportunity to gain experience in taking-off and landing during each flight. Rodney Pyke was to make this take-off.

When the cockpit drill was completed and the engines sufficiently warmed up, Jimmy indicated that Pyke should proceed. The aircraft soon reached flying speed and became airborne. At an altitude of about 50 feet, Pyke signalled and Jimmy raised the undercarriage. The plane was still flying normally. During an initial climb after take-off the altimeter gives the best indication of the plane's progress towards a safe altitude. In the light of subsequent events it would seem that neither Woods nor Pyke attached sufficient importance to this instrument. Instinctively, though, Jimmy must have felt the plane was climbing a little fast because he applied gentle pressure to the control column. Pyke took note of this and made the necessary correction. It was then, so Pyke recalled later, that he felt the aircraft was not behaving normally and was sinking. Jimmy took over complete control of the plane; visibility was nil and they were certainly going down.

When the plane first bumped the ground, Hamersley thought they had hit a wireless mast and told the passengers to brace themselves in case of a crash landing. Pyke was sure a crash landing was inevitable. He recalled thinking at the time, 'I'm going to die, and so far from home'. Jimmy was certain the port engine had failed. What had actually happened was that on initial contact with the ground there had been a drop in engine power as the airscrews scraped in the earth. Woods, trying to regain height, pulled the control column back, causing the aircraft — which was still travelling well above stalling speed — to leap over the buildings of the town before losing speed and plunging into the mangroves. Was it instinct or was it skill? One thing is certain — damage to property was averted and lives saved. Everything had happened very quickly; and at the time of the crash there was no thought of reasons why. Survival was the primary concern; getting the passengers out of the plane in case of fire, then removing mail, freight and luggage from a rising tide.

Forty years later Alec Whitham still recalled the details of that morning vividly. It was still not light when Jimmy took off:

> I walked over to the edge of the runway to watch him go because there was quite a lot of fog around and when he took off past us I could see the white tail light in the fog. It then disappeared. Then we could hear the engine note change. If you remember, the Lockheed Electra 10A take-off noise was very very loud. They used to really scream, and this thing was screaming away. The next minute there was a thump and then complete silence. Of course we knew what had happened, he'd gone down, but no fire, which was quite surprising, because it was full of fuel. Then we got into a jeep and went down to try and locate him.

Fortunately it was low-tide and the mud as well as the leafy mangroves had cushioned the impact. There were no serious casualties, though both Woods and Pyke had minor injuries and Jimmy spent the next three days in the Broome hospital.

By coincidence Mollie Woods was lying in bed in the same hospital when the plane roared overhead. She had gone to Broome for a holiday and was to have joined Jimmy on his ill-fated flight. The afternoon before, while walking with friends along the Broome jetty, Mollie had jumped over the side for a lark, expecting to land on a ledge a few feet below. Instead she plunged 30 feet,

Jimmy's crash, Broome, 1946. The damaged Electra has been removed from Mangroves.

landing in the mud and damaging her spine.

'Thank God it was low tide', she recalled much later. 'Because I couldn't swim. We both owed our lives to the mud.'

She was taken to hospital and a disappointed Jimmy visited her that evening. Shortly before dawn on the following morning she was awakened by a commotion in the corridor as the matron called for towels and bed linen.

'There's been a plane crash', she said. 'Your Jim's down in the sea.'

'Don't be ridiculous', said Mollie. 'He can't be.'

Meanwhile, at the crash site, efforts were being made to salvage as much as possible before high-tide at 11am. Alec Whitham gave instructions to shift instruments, radio gear and other moveable equipment. Horry Miller, who was in Broome at the time, arrived at the site while this was going on and arranged for the plane itself to be dragged onto the beach above the water-line. It was beyond hope of economic repair.

Because there had been no loss of life the crash did not attract a great deal of publicity and was probably soon forgotten except by those who were directly involved. However, there were serious repercussions for Jimmy. The day after the crash the Department of Civil Aviation began an enquiry into its causes, and the finding two weeks later held James Woods totally responsible, firstly for taking off in fog contrary to MMA's operations manual instructions, and secondly for allowing Pyke to attempt an instrument take-off in unsuitable conditions. His Commercial Pilot's Licence was suspended.

It looked as though Jimmy's career as a commercial pilot was in jeopardy. Renewal of his licence meant further tests, especially with regard to instrument flying; although reference had been made to his very fine past record in the findings of the enquiry, his age was seen as factor against renewal. After a lifetime devoted to flying, without a single accident involving loss of life, it seemed a harsh penalty. Yet DCA also had its responsibilities, especially to the flying public. Its rules, though sometimes regarded as draconian, especially by more experienced pilots, were safeguards, mainly against human error. Irritating though they may have been, they were necessary.

How much Jimmy suffered as a result of this finding will never be known. He confided in no one, not even Mollie, and made no reference to the accident or the findings in his diaries or letters. On the face of it, he appeared to have erased the whole unfortunate episode from his mind and simply got on with the process of living. Yet the subsequent events, for which the accident itself was only the catalyst, were to change the whole course of his life.

WOODSIE

Mollie and Jimmy studying the route for the 1953 Air Race.

WOODS AIRWAYS

He was the last man to fly a plane and do everything; pilot, radio officer and engineer.

William Duff

In the weeks following the crash of the Lockheed at Broome, Jimmy had plenty of time to think. Apart from the few days spent in the Broome hospital, he had a short spell in The Mount Hospital in Perth for treatment of a hernia brought about by the crash. No doubt during this period of enforced rest he reviewed his life and pondered the future, though it is unlikely that at the time he contemplated a career other than with MMA. Although his licence had been suspended, he had every reason to assume that it would be reinstated in due course and that he would continue as MMA's route manager, filling in where necessary as pilot. It soon became obvious that this was not the situation. The renewal of his licence was subject to certain conditions and if he flew at all it was to be as first officer rather than captain. The antagonism between Jimmy and Cyril Kleinig had not been resolved either; if anything it had been exacerbated by the Broome crash.

Among his colleagues there was a good deal of sympathy for Jimmy because he was well-liked, but there was also the feeling that it was inevitable, sooner or later, that his flying methods would land him in trouble. Yet it seemed unlikely that any kind of compromise as far as techniques were concerned would be acceptable to him. In his own mind his flying skills were in no way diminished, although he had to acknowledge that he could not adjust to new methods; nor would he be prepared to accept orders from Cyril Kleinig, who was being given, or assuming, more and more responsibility and power all the time.

After coming out of hospital Jimmy went back to work, confined to the ground because of the suspended licence. He became increasingly unhappy with the situation but kept his concerns to himself, not wanting to cause Mollie any worry. He may have seemed a rather 'close' person for this reason, but he was not introverted: he was not one to brood. Yet during the latter part of 1946 he must have wondered how it would all end; how things would finally be resolved.

On 31 December 1946, Cyril Gare signed a letter on behalf of the Managing Director of MMA giving official notice of the company's termination of Jimmy's services. When he received it early in January, Jimmy was shocked and hurt, but replied with typical understatement:

> . . . I must say this information came as a bit of a shock considering I have given over thirteen years of my aviation career with your company, to help build up the Nor-West service to its present state . . .

For a man of different temperament, the pressures of the previous months might have led to tragic consequences. There had been the accident, its cause and implications, the suspension of his licence, the drop in status, and the apparently insoluble problem brought about by the clash of two strong personalities; and now — his dismissal. But Jimmy was not a tragic figure: he was a survivor.

He sought an interview with Horry Miller to clarify the matter of his retirement allowance, reminding Horry of the original terms and conditions of his employment when he had been told that his retirement allowance would be calculated according to the period of his service at the rate of 9 pounds 10 shillings per week. After the interview there were several letters back and forth before the matter was resolved. Jimmy eventually received 800 pounds from MMA on the understanding that he would not compete

142

directly or indirectly with the company. An agreement to this effect was drawn up legally with Olney & Neville acting for MMA and Nicholson & Nicholson for Woods.

Telling Mollie was difficult and it seemed to her that Jamie had been badly let down. She had only just learnt, at a dinner party, that Cyril Kleinig had been made Assistant Manager of MMA. Her immediate reaction was that the job which should have been Jamie's had been given to someone else and that this was the real reason behind his leaving the company. When she expressed these feelings, rather vehemently, Jimmy's quiet reply was 'Don't be bitter, Mollie'.

The next few months tested Jimmy's optimism and resilience. He was not prepared to retire, but under the circumstances what were the alternatives?

He considered his options, balancing the things he could and would do against those he could not or would not come to terms with. He was an excellent VFR pilot. He had more than 30 years experience flying a variety of planes, but small planes suited him best. He was also a resourceful and competent mechanic, and although he may have thought about his early years working at George Abel's garage, and acting as chauffeur to the well-to-do, he could not imagine working with petrol pumps and tuning up engines for the rest of his life. Anyway, Perth in the late 1940s had few calls for chauffeur-driven cars and he certainly never seriously considered such an idea. But the possibility of a business of his own was something else. He remembered the plans he and Dick de Lisle had once had to provide joy-rides and a mail service in New Zealand. And he remembered the attempts he had made to provide an air service to the Shetlands and Orkneys from Aberdeen in Scotland in partnership with William Hadden. Perhaps something like that was a possibility. Of course he would need financial backing to undertake such a project, and it would need to be a realistic venture; the public could no longer be persuaded to part with 5 pounds for a flip above the city, and mail services were provided by larger airlines.

Round and round went the ideas in his head. What sort of service? And where to? Somewhere that could be reached easily in daylight hours. He would have nothing more to do with IFR — in any case, under the terms of his reinstated licence he would only be permitted to fly by VFR.

Then it came to him ... holidays, fun, short hops ... to Rottnest and Garden islands, where many Perth people headed for vacation. He would provide a service to both resorts, and possibly a newspaper delivery service to the south-west of the State as well. Already there was a service to Rottnest provided by Charlie Snook, but Jimmy was confident that the traffic would warrant a competitor. The islands were only minutes flying time from the mainland. He could fly a shuttle service. It would be a boon for the public and a money-spinner for him.

For Mollie, the realisation that there was no longer security of a well-paid job and that Jamie was not simply on extended leave, had hit hard. Now, the prospect of his running his own airline, while in some ways exciting, was also bewildering in terms of the demands it would make on them both. Although she was by nature fatalistic, there were times when she would explode if something upset her. She recalled on this occasion threatening to drown herself in the river.

Jimmy remained calm.

'Don't forget to take a cake of soap with you', he replied.

Another woman might have been further enraged by such a response, but Mollie, who could never stay mad at Jamie for long, burst out laughing, and said that if it was Jamie's choice then she accepted it.

Jimmy's next step was to apply for an air service licence and on 22 July 1947 he received a letter from the Secretary of the Western Australian Transport Board:

> I have pleasure in advising that approval has been granted to your application for an air service licence to operate between Perth and Rottnest and Garden Island for the transport of passengers and freight and from Perth and various south-west and great southern towns for the purpose of delivery of newspapers.

The letter also pointed out that the actual licence could not be issued until details of planes had been supplied and that it was up to Jimmy to provide full particulars after he had purchased the aircraft.

While working out the details of his proposed airline service,

144

Jimmy had been in touch with Jim McCartney of West Australian Newspapers to enquire about the possibility of a contract to transport newspapers to south-west and great-southern towns. Jimmy had always had a good relationship with the press, not only because of his newsworthiness. He had often gone out of his way to deliver newspapers when flying over the remote parts of Western Australia. There is no doubt that Jimmy saw his proposed service as one which would bring mutual benefit.

With the groundwork laid, he set about looking for suitable aircraft. He needed at least two if he was to provide a regular service and they would have to be small planes and ones with which he was familiar. Among the MMA fleet were several Avro Ansons — war surplus planes that had not been converted for passenger use and were obsolete with the expansion of the company's services and the use of larger planes. Jimmy was able to purchase three with some spare parts for approximately 1500 pounds. Conversion costs and a motor vehicle for transport of passengers increased the total outlay to 4061 pounds and five pence.

Somehow Jimmy had to raise this sum. His infectious enthusiasm soon had the solid support of a number of friends and acquiantances: Dr Hector Stewart, Leonard Day, Bertram Nairn and Hamish MacMillan, Margaret Stewart, accountant John MacCauley, and lawyer John Nicholson, as well as George Gooch, Ben Sharp and the Atwood Motor Company. Many were prepared to offer financial backing and that cleared the way for Jimmy to pursue the purchase of aircraft.

He also wrote again to McCartney explaining his plans in more detail and pointing out that if he secured a contract with WA Newspapers, he would convert a third plane for the carriage of newspapers. But the real purpose behind his letter was to see if WA Newspapers would be interested in subscribing to the venture. On this occasion they were not prepared to become financially involved and so some of the original group of supporters, together with Mollie and Jimmy became the founding shareholders of the company, Woods Airways Pty Ltd. It was registered on 4 December 1947, with Jimmy as Managing Director, William Duff as Chairman of Directors and John McAuley as Company Secretary. The registered office of the company was in the premises of accountants Duff and McAuley at 88 St George's Terrace, Perth.

John Nicholson drew up the Articles of Association and Memorandum of the Company and worked out detailed costings. It was all well thought through: licence fees, running and maintenance costs, charges for hangar space, fire insurance and passenger services (which included promotion of the new airline, the printing of tickets and transport to and from the airport). The additional costs that were to emerge meant that Jimmy had a constant battle to balance his books. It also meant considerable change in lifestyle. Mollie, in the past, had been able to pursue her own interests, confident of Jamie's support, financially and in every other way. Now she became an active partner in the business, and when the service was established she would often drive passengers to and from Maylands. It was a measure of the strength of their relationship that it survived what must have been difficult and unexpected pressures. Jimmy, with his way of tackling each problem as it arose, cutting his losses when necessary and always thinking positively, proved that his Scottish stoicism and tenacity paid off in the long run; Mollie, with her good spirits and cheerfulness, provided the antidote he needed when things looked grim.

The service commenced as planned on the weekend of Easter 5 March 1948, operating a twice-weekly flight from Maylands to Rottnest and return (a distance of approximately 22 miles), with additional flights as custom demanded. (Garden Island and the South-West newspaper delivery service had been abandoned). The fare was one pound each way with a maximum possible revenue for each flight of 14 pounds: the average return was something like 7 pounds.

Because the company received no subsidy Jimmy had to look carefully at every means of keeping expenses to a minimum. This was to lead to further conflict with DCA.

Taking a flight with 'Woodsie' was always something of an adventure. He sold the tickets (or, if you were lucky, 'the lovely Mrs W' did) and helped the passengers with their baggage which was stowed in the back of the Ford station wagon. The passengers piled in and were driven to Maylands at breakneck speed. 'You were safer in the air with Woodsie than you ever were on the ground', said one former traveller. At the airport Jimmy carried the bags to the aircraft and shoved them aboard, accepted the

WOODS AIRWAYS PTY. LTD.

The Smallest Scheduled Air Line Route in the World

————o—O—o————

Perth .. .. *Rottnest Island*

National House ... 49 William St,, Perth ... Western Australia

Phones :- BA 6504 - BA 7393 - - After hours BA 3013

PASSENGER TO ROTTNEST

M..

....LDS.................................

Woods Airways in business, 1948.

previously purchased tickets, organised seating arrangements, and made sure he had someone dependable (and reasonably strong) in the front seat next to him. It was this person's job to switch on the ignition key while Jimmy swung the propeller. He would then climb aboard and once the plane was airborne, turn to the passenger beside him and elicit his help. Paul Rigby, cartoonist with the *Daily News* at the time, made many trips with Jimmy. According to Rigby, Jimmy would:

> ... jab his finger at the winch alongside my right hand. This meant 129 turns by hand of this primitive grinder to raise the heaviest aircraft undercart known to man. Somewhere beyond Gage Roads I would have sweatily completed the task and slumped back in the nav's seat. Jimmy didn't even take the pipe out of his mouth and indicated the winch again. Another 129 turns to get the bloody thing down again, and 'do it quick! we're about to land!'

If Jimmy had thought that all his problems would be solved when he ran his own airline and reverted to visual flying only, he was quite mistaken. The flying part presented no real problems, though one or two incidents served to remind him that there were always hazards connected to the aircraft industry. Instead, it was bureaucracy that caused him problems. There are people who live

147

'It's justa hop!' Promotional poster.

by rules, at ease only within the framework of regulations — the parameters of what is possible are set. Jimmy Woods was not this kind of person. Rules were not necessarily made to be broken, but they could certainly be stretched or adapted to suit different situations; although Jimmy was essentially an easy going man and never deliberately sought confrontation, there was something in his nature that thrived on tension. Once, this had been satisfied by the challenges of lone flight — pitting himself against nature, or getting a grounded plane airborne. Now it seemed almost as if he enjoyed the setting of himself, the individual, against the forces of officialdom.

For years Jimmy had had minor confrontations with the Department of Civil Aviation, mainly about his failture to submit logbooks on demand, or his late renewal of licences. The suspension of his licence after the Broome accident had been the only serious penalty he had incurred. He was soon to discover a new and frustrating world of regulations and red tape. The regulations in themselves were reasonable. They were laid down in the interests of air safety and it was important that they be observed. However, the implementation of some of the minor details often preoccupied departmental officers. Certainly some went out of their way to be helpful, but others engaged in what seemed to become a personal vendetta against the maverick Jimmy Woods, and these confrontations became legendary, with the media always siding with Jimmy who was seen as the lone individual taking on the might of a whole government department.

A month after the inaugural flight of Woods Airways, Jimmy received notification from the Superintendent of Airports that he would have to transfer his operations from Maylands to Guildford by 1 May 1948. It was suggested that if he needed accommodation for office space or passenger handling, it might be possible to make available part of the building formerly used by MMA as a passenger lounge. On the face of it, it seemed a reasonable proposition but for Jimmy the implications were quite serious. There was no hangar space for his aircraft at Guildford and it was impractical for them to be left in the open. Also, it was much further to transfer passengers from Perth to Guildford than to Maylands. Jimmy ignored the instruction. There was no immed-

149

iate reaction from the Department and he continued from Maylands as before.

It was not long before another incident caused further Departmental concern.

In having the Ansons converted for the carriage of passengers, Jimmy had some minor adjustments made to allow him to start the plane with passenger assistance. There was always a good deal of passenger involvement in Woods Airways. As well as co-opting a willing passenger to wind the winch that retracted the wheels, Jimmy would get someone to operate the ignition switch while he manually turned the airscrews. This worked quite well. However, on the morning of 13 November 1948, having elicited the co-operation of one of the passengers to attend the switch, Jimmy prepared to turn the propeller. It spun prematurely and sliced into his buttock. He was rushed to Royal Perth Hospital, bleeding copiously. Meanwhile, an astonished Mollie opened the front door of the Arbordale flat to a young employee of the company who said he had come for Captain Woods' pyjamas.

One of the young medical registrars at the hospital, Ken Bellemore, recalled the subsequent events 40 years later:

> . . . he was quite shocked and had precious little time to be stoical or anxious as he was quickly moved to the operating theatre where I repaired this large wound under a general anaesthetic given by the medical registrar . . . at one stage he stopped breathing but we managed to get him going again He was very shocked and needed careful resuscitation.
>
> . . . Later that afternoon Mr Bert Nairn [Senior Surgeon] rang and asked me who had operated on Jimmy Woods. I informed him . . . and he said 'Please contact me if you need any help'.
>
> A short time later Mr Eric Kyle [Senior Surgeon] and several others rang with the same query and offered to help if required.
>
> I was met later by the other Registrar who had given the anaesthetic and he said in a shocked tone, 'Do you know whom we have just operated on?' 'No', I replied. 'Well, it's Jimmy Woods of Woods Airways and a close friend of practically all the surgeons on the hospital staff . . . I hope you managed to preserve the sciatic nerve before sewing him up.'
>
> With that I took him back to the patient's bed and lifting

150

Jimmy and Mollie's home, 1939-1971.

the corners I exposed his feet and on stroking the soles his big toes on both sides shot up . . .

He was apparently pleased with our care as he shouted us all a trip to Rottnest . . .

Jimmy was lucky to have got off so lightly, but DCA took a serious view of the incident. One of its officers received written direction:

Please inform Woods that we definitely require to have a pilot in the cockpit at the controls when engines are being started for flight. His practice of starting up himself is to cease forthwith. Please confirm this requirement has been made known to Woods and check that it is being complied with at both terminals.

The following month there were other minor complaints about overloading and pre-flight tests. Jimmy calculated passenger weight at 170 pounds for males and 120 pounds for females. The Department required exact weights or averaging out at 170 pounds, regardless of sex. As far as the pre-flight tests were concerned, Jimmy replied with a lengthy letter, pointing out that if:

the ACO and others had been more alert . . . they would have heard my motors being tested before take-off, but owing to the strong wind this may not have been possible. I would like to point out that owing to the soft nature of the extreme ends of the runways . . . it has been my procedure to check . . . on the rundown to avoid blowing runway into the sea and all through the aircraft, which is very detrimental . . .

Jimmy became increasingly irritated by what seemed to be nit-picking complaints and he frequently ignored attempts by DCA to communicate with him.

Dorothy White, who was employed by Duff & McAuley but also acted as Jimmy's secretary, recalled Jimmy's reaction when she reminded him that DCA wanted to speak to him urgently. (The DCA office was down the passage in the same building).

'I haven't got time. I've got a plane to fly', said Jimmy, and disappeared out of the door.

By July 1949 the question of Guildford versus Maylands arose again with a stern injunction.

> As from 1st August you are to conduct all operations covered
> by this airline licence from Guildford airport and not from
> Maylands.

Jimmy had already won more than a year's respite since
receiving the first instruction to transfer. Now a paper war was to
begin in earnest between Woods Airways and the Department of
Civil Aviation.

In one of many letters dealing with the subject, Jimmy wrote to
the Regional Director of DCA in Western Australia, David Ross,
pointing out that in spite of extensive enquiries he could not find
suitable accommodation for his company's planes at Guildford.
Not being a subsidised company, Woods Airways, was unable to
raise the capital to build a hangar. He asked DCA to reverse its
decision, but added that he would try to find accommodation at
Guildford as soon as possible.

There was no immediate reply to that letter; instead the
Department resorted to other tactics, pointing out that the length
of take-off at Maylands was insufficient. Were there no other
suitable aerodrome then Maylands would be acceptable, but with
Guildford so close such concession could not be made. They had
an alternative solution however, suggesting that Woods Airways
planes be housed at Maylands, fly to Guildford each morning to
pick up passengers, and on the last return-trip of the day land at
Maylands (with passengers).

Jimmy pointed out the difficulties and inconvenience of such
an arrangement and correspondence continued between the two
organisations. The file bulged with letters, telegrams and inter-
office memos, and Jimmy's delaying tactics paid off. By 1
December 1949 he was still operating out of Maylands.

It was time for the Department to resort to stronger tactics. In
December 1949, Ross notified his Head Office of an instruction
demanding Woods Airways transfer to Guildford, adding, 'I think
that this instruction will be ignored and would like your advice on
action to be taken in this event'.

By 16 December moves were underway to prosecute Jimmy for
defiance of the Department's instructions and it is at this point
that the situation took on almost comic overtones. DCA discovered

that Jimmy's airline licence — which should have been despatched from DCA headquarters after renewal — had either been held up or lost in the post, and that in the absence of a licence it had no power to prosecute. In a letter to Jimmy dated 9 January 1950, using bluff tactics, it was pointed out that, nevertheless, the Department had no option but to take action if the transfer was not made forthwith.

On 12 January, Jimmy was interviewed by Departmental Officer Earl Fry, but still maintained that he would not move his operations to Guildford. The Department had another couple of cards up its sleeve. It claimed that Woods was contravening regulations by flying without a radio and that he was overloading his aircraft. A passage from a lengthy report covering all possible causes for complaint gives a clue to the power struggle that had been behind the exercise:

> The continued lack of observance of Departmental directions and orders by this Company, which up to the present time has been blithely carrying on these unsatisfactory operations, is considered to be detrimental to the authority of the officers of this Region over other operating companies.

Finally, when Woods' airline licence turned up, the Department was able to take legal action and Jimmy was forced to capitulate. In a telegram from Melbourne on 13 March 1950, the matter appeared to be officially concluded:

> Woods is now willing to comply with Departmental requirements and [the Minister] has agreed to withold prosecution on that understanding.

A second condition to the dropping of legal action against the company was that Woods Airways should fit its aircraft with radio as quickly as possible. Jimmy made enquiries of AWA in Sydney about the cost of installation of radio and was quoted a figure of 580 pounds. In a lengthy letter to DCA subsequently he explained that:

> When we considered installing radio we did not anticipate it would be so expensive, and unless your Department can see some way in helping us out of our difficulty, our Directors regret to state that our resources cannot yet meet such a

154

commitment.

He went on to explain that there had been no difficulty with control tower signals at Guildford and that his scheduled times did not coincide with other operators. There was silence for a while from DCA on that matter because another infringement was occupying its attention.

One of the Ansons, on landing at Guildford, had suffered damage to the pitot head (part of the system for indicating air speed) and the propellers. While awaiting replacement parts the aircraft was housed in one of the MMA hangars, but had to be moved out onto the tarmac to make room for an MMA plane. On the weekend of 22-23 April, the spare propellers having arrived, Jimmy set about fitting them. It started to rain; because he was anxious to get the plane to Maylands as soon as possible and had already notified the Departmental inspector of his intention of ferrying the plane across. Jimmy took off as soon as the propellers were in place. He did not have a spare pitot head so flew with the unserviceable one.

Jimmy landed safely; the pitot head was replaced and he put the incident out of his mind. Not so DCA. He was called to explain why he had flown in contravention of the air navigation regulation without application being made to ferry. The subsequent exchange between Jimmy and airworthiness inspector Fred Brookman, as related by the then Regional Director Bob Pritchard, offers some light relief:

> Fred Brookman: Well, you know, how come you flew the aeroplane and it was unairworthy?
> Jimmy Woods: No it wasn't.
> Fred: Yes it was. You flew over without any air speed indicator.
> Jimmy: Fred, I wasn't going anywhere so I didn't want to work out how long it was going to take me.

Then the question of radio installation cropped up again and Jimmy made enquiries from Amalgamated Wireless, Australasia, about an Airmight installation at lower cost than the quote he had received from AWA. He suggested that the Department might approve the alternative.

The Department was not impressed:

155

> It is considered that this company [Woods Airways] is merely stalling for time and if, as is expected, this present request [AWA] is refused they will then stall further by submitting a request to install an Airmight.

Jimmy was certainly stalling, but for good reason. Five hundred and eighty pounds would have crippled the company financially. But he had bought time. On 24 August he was instructed that the radio apparatus must be installed by 1 November 1950. In spite of the additional time allowed, on 16 October Woods wrote to the Director General of DCA:

> ... we regret we are not in a position financially to meet such a heavy burden since we are not in receipt of any subsidy ... we have not yet been able to strike any dividend for our shareholders and unless we get relief from this unwarranted expenditure we will be unable to carry on.

The Regional Director, David Ross, supported Woods. In an attempt to intercede on his behalf with the Department he wrote to Head Office, saying that it was his personal opinion that the fitting of radio for operations solely to and from Rottnest was hardly essential, especially as all other aircraft from Guildford were fitted with radios. His letter continued:

> We are now faced with a policy decision as to whether fitting of radios for this very short air service of 25 miles is of sufficient importance to put a small operator out of business.

Ross's plea did not go down very well with the Director General of Civil Aviation, Carn Wiggins, who pointed out that a special procedure for the needs of one airline was not a sound arrangement and that Woods Airways had the only regular public transport aircraft in Australia that did not carry radio.

The correspondence continued while Jimmy flew on, radioless. On 13 April 1951 he was again instructed to have radio fitted, this time by 1 June. On 4 May Jimmy told the Regional Director he would not fit radio and that the Department's instruction left him no alternative but to sell his aircraft and go out of business. Wiggins called his bluff; on 13 June Woods' Airline licence (No. 217) was cancelled. Jimmy was told that if he continued to operate he would be liable for prosecution.

Rottnest showing airstrip.

Jimmy could hold out no longer. Somehow he raised the money, agreed to fit the radios and suspension was withdrawn. Some officers of the Department may have felt Jimmy's delaying tactics were mere bloody-mindedness. They were not (although Jimmy may have gained some perverse humour and satisfaction from the exercise). He was fighting for economic survival and every month of delay was a month of operation gained.

While all these battles were going on Jimmy was flying back and forth to Rottnest, offering safe and reliable passage, his confidence unshaken and always genial to his passengers. The number of his personal friends and admirers, many of them influential, grew and grew.

MOSQUITO IN THE HANGAR

Jim said, 'I've got a Mosquito in the hangar and a little spitfire at home!'

Mollie Woods

Just when the idea of entering the 1953 New Zealand Air Race occurred to Jimmy is not clear, but undoubtedly he would have read reports of the proposed race with its speed and handicap sections. His early links with New Zealand and his entry in the 1934 Air Race may well have fired his interest. Or perhaps he simply needed a break from the attentions and constant vigilance of DCA officers who were ever on the lookout for some breach. It seemed almost as if they were out to 'get' him, to put him out of business, and it would not have been surprising if he had felt victimised. Instead, unflappable, he stalled and bluffed and laughed up his sleeve at some of the complaints that were laid against him. For their part, many of the officers pursued their duties more with regret than any other emotion — sorry to have to hound someone they were basically very fond of. Some went out of their way to help Jimmy overcome official obstacles, because they knew that with his stubborn nature and determination he would pursue whatever course he was on: with their cooperation they could ensure that risks were avoided.

Apart from this tension (in some ways self-caused), there were

Jimmy with the Mosquito.

few challenges for Jimmy in those years. Back and forth he flew over that 12-mile stretch of water. Take-off and land; unload baggage; transport passengers; exchange tickets for money; load-up and take-off again. It was a flying bus service and unexciting except for the contact with interesting and varied people.

The only real diversion in the first few years of Woods Airways operations was in September 1952, when Jimmy was engaged by the WA Newspapers to fly a team of photographers to record the atomic explosion on the Monte Bello group of islands off the north-west coast of Western Australia.

Jimmy flew the men to Mardie Station near Onslow, where he and his co-pilot would be accommodated while the 'press gang' camped at a site 24 miles north. For the next couple of weeks Jimmy made entries in his diary, something he had not done for a long time:

> . . . climbed to the top of Nick's Knob to view some of the Monte Bello group and saw all the battery of cameras where the great pictures were to be taken.
> . . . nobody knows when the THING may go off.

Each evening he concluded his day's record with a fond message for Mollie.

He amused himself at the station by helping with fencing, visiting the windmills, tying up the vines on the homestead balcony, shooting kangaroos and crows (and missing the wild turkeys), and going net fishing. The plane's engines had to be checked daily and the weather was perfect. He was obviously enjoying a much needed break ... 'I have just forgotten there was a Woods' Air Service to Rottnest', he wrote. In that North West environment he could well have forgotten the intervening years, too, and felt that he was a young man again.

The days slipped past, yet the bomb was never quite ignored. The station people took down all their pictures in case they were dislodged by the explosion. There seemed to be no real concern about the genetic effects of the release of radioactive dust though Jimmy did comment at one stage that 'there was too much wind for the bomb to go off — westerly would blow radioactive smoke over land'. Mostly he referred to it as 'the THING'. When it was actually detonated his comment was quite without irony:

> Mardie. Friday 2nd October 1952. The Atomic bomb was heard by us at Mardie at 08-04 just after breakfast.

Then, their commission completed, the photographers climbed aboard the plane and Jimmy took off for Perth, noting while at the controls that the atomic cloud was still visible at 11.10am as they flew over Onslow at 4,000 feet.

Jimmy's break from routine and the excitement of being involved with the press team may have unsettled him, or it may simply have been coincidence, but it was after this trip that he began making serious attempts to procure a Mosquito aircraft for entry in the New Zealand air race. The RAAF had a number of obsolescent war surplus Mosquito aircraft, some of which had already been acquired by companies for high-altitude charter work. The Government had also made a gift of one to ex-Squadron Leader A J R Oates to fly in the race, provided he undertook to have it overhauled at his own expense.

Paul Hasluck, then Minister for Territories, made representations on Jimmy's behalf to William McMahon, Minister for Air, to see if one could be made available for Jimmy to also compete.

The 1953 air race was planned to cover a course similar to the Great Air Race of 1934 but would finish in Christchurch instead of Melbourne. With greater speed and range, the planes would need fewer refuelling stops than in the former race, and it was expected that the winner of the speed section would complete the journey in less than 24 hours. The object of the race was primarily to promote New Zealand. More idealistically, the aim was also to further the interests of international goodwill and understanding, and to make New Zealanders aware of the advances in civil aviation. In addition it would give aircraft manufacturers and airline operators a chance to display their goods and services.

Even at 60 Jimmy could be tempted by the idea of breaking a record, and if he did not win the race he would have the satisfaction of knowing he was the only entrant in the speed section who had also competed in the 1934 event. Many of those former entrants were dead; killed in crashes or during the war. Others, like his navigator DC Bennett, who was a very high-ranking officer in the RAF, had long given up the adventures that attracted younger men. Age, it seemed to Jimmy, was no barrier; an attitude of mind, experience and instinct more than compensated for slightly slower reactions.

Before he pursued the matter of the Mosquito aircraft any further with the Government, he had to find a financial backer for the venture. This time WA Newspapers was prepared to help and Jimmy replied to the Minister for Air confirming his interest. On 4 March 1953 he received a telegram from Paul Hasluck saying that the plane would be made available to him for the nominal sum of 100 pounds. Jimmy sent a cheque, provided by WA Newspapers, and agreed to take delivery of the aircraft from the RAAF base in Queensland.

The transaction was concluded with a letter from the Department of Supply setting out conditions of sale. The aircraft was being made available only on the condition that it be used specifically for participation in the air race. Woods was not to dispose of it prior to the conclusion of the race, nor subsequently without obtaining Government approval. The sale was finally completed on 20 March 1953.

The aircraft needed considerable work done on it before it would be serviceable enough to fly in the race. This work would be done at the de Havilland facility in Sydney, and to fly it there Jimmy had to have a Certificate of Airworthiness. In the plane's present state this would never be given. Again he approached Paul Hasluck to intercede on his behalf with the Minister for Air. Jimmy's file with Federal Ministers grew and grew.

The RAAF would need to spend 250 man-hours to get the Mosquito serviceable enough to fly to Sydney, if no additional faults showed up. But they were prepared to do this, even though, so they said, it would be at the expense of servicing their own aircraft which were needed for 'warlike operations' in Malaya. The Minister said he would authorise the work provided Jimmy could get a statement from DCA that they would licence him and his crew for the flight from England to New Zealand. Approval depended upon a Certificate of Airworthiness being granted for overhaul at the de Havilland facility. DCA made this undertaking, and in June Jimmy flew to Sydney to make the necessary arrangements for the overhaul. With entry in the race now much more of a reality he rang Jim McCartney to bring him up to date. A couple of days later he flew home.

By early September the aircraft was ready and its Certificate of Airworthiness approved. Jimmy flew to Amberley RAAF base near Brisbane where the Mosquito awaited him. Soon after arrival he wrote:

> ... I was shown over my Mossie. She looked very nice and I also met F/L Max Galloway ... took the Mossie up for a flight over Moreton Island ... I enjoyed every minute of it. I was shown the various arrangements for fuel operations, running on one motor and various procedures. Then we came in for a landing at 125 KN which seemed easy enough, but all requires a little practice.

The next morning Galloway took Jimmy for another couple of circuits, then in the afternoon, after some deliberations about getting a dual-control Mosquito from Archerfield so that Jimmy could fly solo under supervision (and finding that none would be available for a week), it was decided that Jimmy would make his first solo flight in the Mosquito without an instructor present. Max Galloway, recalling the occasion some years later, said he had some misgiving about letting Jimmy take the aircraft up alone after so short a familiarisation period. But, in his own words:

> ... how can you say to a bloke who has got 25,000 hours that you don't want to send him up solo? So we all got out of the road and sent him off. He did a couple of circuits and came in and landed.

Jimmy's own recollections were more detailed:

> ... about 4 o'clock I started up the two Rolls Royce motors [they were actually Packard-Merlin engines] and took off on my first solo and after flying around for a bit I came in and made a very nice landing. Then I went for another one and came in a bit faster but still made a good landing ... I felt quite confident that I would justify the confidence of my instructor ... they seemed so surprised [my] coming off Ansons and not having flown anything faster since '47 that I should do so well so the C.O. said it must be the result of being a teetotaler.

Some of his colleagues in Perth had also been apprehensive because, according to Bob Pritchard of DCA, the Mosquito was 'a real hot rod' and could be quite dangerous on take-off.

By the time Jimmy had ferried the plane across the country to Perth with Max Galloway, his total flying time in the Mosquito was 14 hours. His licence was endorsed for Mosquito MK41 type aircraft and valid for day flying only until 31 October 1953.

Although Jimmy was back safely with his aircraft (which he had named 'The Quokka') Mollie realised how worried she was about his proposed venture, though she kept such concerns to herself. She knew what was being said about the Mosquito and she also knew the kind of stress Jimmy would be under during the race. Jimmy had no such misgivings. He was more excited than he had been for years. Everything seemed to be going well; he was just awaiting final confirmation of sponsorship.

Less than a fortnight before the start of the race Jim McCartney rang — WA Newspapers had withdrawn its sponsorship. Mollie would never forget that phone call.

'Jamie put the phone down', she said, 'and burst into tears. I had never seen him do such a thing before.'

The probable reason for the withdrawal was that Canberra jets (some of which were competing in the race) had been breaking

163

records and it seemed unlikely that a Mosquito would be able to match their speed. It was just not worth the gamble.

Mollie was relieved, feeling that the decision was for the best. She was convinced that if Jamie flew in that race she would never see him again. But Jimmy had not given up. Two days after the shock of McCartney's phone call, he arranged an interview with a visiting Sydney philanthropist, Sir Edward Hallstrom, and attempted to interest him in sponsoring the Mosquito. Sir Edward promised to give a definite reply within a few days. Jimmy waited anxiously, knowing that Sir Edward had returned to Sydney. For three days he waited and on the third evening, unable to stand the suspense any longer, he rang Sir Edward at his Sydney home. There was no reply. The next day he received a telegram saying that there was insufficient time to arrange race sponsorship. He wrote in his diary:

> Well, that's that. Most disappointed, but glad for Mollie's sake. But she was so brave about it all along, nor would she have stopped me and all through my flying career she has been the gamest and [most] sensible woman in the world.

He called London and New Zealand withdrawing his entry in the race. The Mosquito was struck off the registrar and its provisional certificate of Airworthiness suspended.

By coincidence, just before Jim McCartney passed on WA Newspapers' decision, Jimmy had received a letter from the general manager of Sepal, distributing agents in Sydney. The company was aware that Jimmy had ferried a Mosquito aircraft to Western Australia and had a client who was interested in purchasing it. At the time Jimmy had not bothered to follow up the enquiry. Now, left with an aircraft for which he had no immediate use, he could see that Sepal's enquiry might be worth pursuing. The Mosquito was originally valued at 60,000 pounds — its disposal price had been nominal only. Although Jimmy had not paid the 100 pounds out of his own pocket, he had undertaken the cost of its overhaul, and sundry other expenses had been incurred — travel and accommodation during the ferrying operations, licence fees and now, hangar costs. He offered the Mosquito to Sepals for 5,000 pounds.

Three weeks later he received a reply:

> We regret to advise that our American friends, although interested in your Mosquito are not prepared to pay the price asked by you, namely £5,000stg.

Negotiations went on, however, on the basis of a lower figure, and on 30 October Jimmy received a cheque on behalf of Sepal for 1,000 pounds as deposit, the balance (2,000 pounds) to be paid on delivery. The cheque was never cashed because the Department of Supply stepped in. This was not because of the original conditions imposed when Jimmy acquired the aircraft, but because of the plane's Lend-Lease Packard-Merlin engines. The United States had an embargo on selling Lend-Lease equipment to American interests, arguing that such items belonged to the United States anyway, Australia never having purchased them. For Jimmy, this was the beginning of another protracted paper war, this time with the Department of Supply.

As the months went by and the cost of hangar space was becoming a burden, Jimmy decided to try once more to sell the Mosquito. He exhausted all avenues, seeking permission to sell to an American buyer, even suggesting that he would be willing to replace the Packard-Merlin engines with Rolls Royce motors, though just how he would finance such a costly operation is not clear. The Government maintained its stand: he could not sell the aircraft. Jimmy's lawyers wrote to the Minister, threatening legal action if Jimmy could not get permission to export the machine. The Department of Supply stood firm. Jimmy then contemplated leasing the machine and in desperation also suggested that the Government could repurchase it for 3,000 pounds. He made representations direct to the Minister of Supply, Howard Beale, and through various official channels, but got nowhere. In fact, the Minister warned that if Jimmy leased out the aircraft, proceedings would be started against *him*.

For several months Jimmy kept up a steady bombardment of the Department. How much it had become a power struggle is hard to say, because Jimmy was certainly out-of-pocket over the whole Mosquito venture.

Finally the Director of Contracts at the Department of Supply wrote to say:

> ... he [the Minister] would never have consented to this plane

being made available at a nominal fee for a specific purpose and no other if he had had the slightest idea that the purpose having failed Capt. Woods would seek to make personal profit out of the Commonwealth's generous treatment.

There is a hint of 'dog in the manger' about this attitude, because it was highly unlikely that the Government would have been able to dispose of war surplus aircraft at anything other than a nominal figure. The letter went on to say that the Government was prepared to repay the purchase price plus reasonable expenses. Jimmy replied saying that they could have it for 2,000 pounds because 'it is taking up space'. The Minister responded (personally this time) in very strong terms, repeating what the Director of Contracts had already said. No sale was concluded.

Jimmy now had more pressing concerns, once again with DCA. The problem of the Mosquito was put aside and the plane remained in the ANA hangar at Guildford while he geared up for a major tussle over infringement of regulations at Rottnest air strip.

DUMMY GUN

In regard to safety, I write the law.

C.S. Wiggins, Department of Civil Aviation

1956 brought about a showdown between Jimmy and DCA, which resulted in demonstration of public support for the man who had become something of a legend in Western Australia.

Having won minor battles over the previous few years — battles of attrition rather than anything else — DCA began to focus all its forces on one particular aspect of Jimmy's waywardness. This was his persistent disregard for their newly-established rule against take-off from the cross-strip at Rottnest into the wind when an easterly was blowing. Head Office in Melbourne had brought in this regulation based on desk-top calculations. It was claimed that there was insufficient distance for safe take-off, a claim that mystified pilots who had been flying in and out of Rottnest for years.

DCA had leased the airstrip from the Rottnest Board of Control for 25 years and it was the Department's responsibility to bring the strip up to international standards; something it had failed to do because of the excessive costs involved. Yet, even though the strip was considered sub-standard, the Department had allowed companies to operate Ansons and other small aircraft from it. There had never been an accident or even a significant mishap during those 25 years.

There were actually two airstrips on Rottnest — the main one, and a cross strip running NE/SW. The latter was the problem. It was claimed that when an easterly wind was blowing, the effective length of this strip was reduced from 3,000 feet to 1,720 feet. Also, because of certain obstructions at either end of the strip — the 70 foot limestone hills near the army barracks at the eastern end and hills nearly 30 feet high at the other — take-off was deemed hazardous.

When Jimmy was informed of the new regulations he asked the Regional Office of DCA to check with Melbourne, believing that there must be some error in the calculations. Ironically, in questioning an apparent anomaly, Jimmy precipitated the cancellation of his licence because it brought attention to the fact that he was disregarding the new regulation — he continued flying, into the easterly wind if necessary, as before. He maintained that the officers in Melbourne had never seen the Rottnest airstrip and that the evidence of his eight years of flying in and out — with DCA permission and experiencing absolutely no difficulties — suggested that DCA had simply made a mistake.

Jimmy's attitude played into the hands of those who felt he had already overstepped the mark. There had been a number of times when, committed to providing the best service possible for his passengers, he had broken the rules. Once, in 1950, he had carried nine passengers when there were seats for only eight. He had made the decision on compassionate grounds — a young man with a carbuncle needed emergency treatment but had no booking for the flight to Perth. Jimmy could have left one of the other passengers behind, or he could have ignored the young man's plight and left him to spend another pain-filled night. Jimmy was sure an extra passenger would not endanger the others and took him aboard. For this he was reprimanded and the breach recorded in his file. In 1955, the wife of a Rottnest Island Board employee went into premature labour and Jimmy decided to risk a take-off at night, assisted by a battery of kerosene lamps. Later the same month, another islander, suffering from acute appendicitis, was air-lifted in a similar way. Jimmy did not think that he was doing anything risky. If he had, he would probably have gone ahead anyway — lives were at stake. And for those people whose lives were in some

168

danger, there was no thought of regulations. They wanted to get to the mainland as quickly and as comfortably as possible. They regarded Jimmy as a hero.

This dedication to his passengers apparently meant nothing to the faceless men in DCA, though there were individuals who admired him for his compassion. But officially, Captain Woods was flouting the Department's authority. Again. And again. And again. Yet there was little they could do, frustrating though it might be, because there had been no accident on which to pin a suspension. Apart from the unfortunate incident with the propeller when Jimmy himself was injured, there had not been a single accident that could be held as evidence of his incompetence. No passenger had ever lodged a complaint — quite the opposite — his passengers were always full of praise. Residents of Rottnest, too, were constantly indebted to Jimmy — for bringing needed stores when ferries couldn't make it because of stormy weather, or simply for getting across to the mainland at short notice. Although this bending of the regulations was a source of irritation to the Department, and some officers found Jimmy's defiance and laid-back style infuriating, there had to be some official basis for action against him.

The new regulation, and Jimmy's decision to ignore it, provided the necessary pretext on which to recommend cancellation of his licence.

On 21 May 1956, an easterly was blowing at Rottnest. Two planes were waiting to take-off for Guildford, each with a full load of passengers. The pilot of the MMA plane decided to abide by the regulations. He off-loaded his passengers and flew back to Guildford with an empty plane. Jimmy ignored the regulation, taking-off into the wind. After landing at Guildford, he turned the plane around and went back for the stranded MMA passengers. On arrival at Guildford the second time, he was asked for an explanation.

'I've had enough of regulations', he said. 'I shall do another flight this afternoon and if the wind's from the east, I'll take off into the wind.'

He said that he would continue to do so until the Department clarified the situation.

On 24 May Jimmy's licence was cancelled for violation of Air

Navigation Rule 227. Woods Airways operations were suspended.

The newspapers carried large headlines and indignant well-wishers rushed into print:

> Captain Woods has never let the Rottnest people down. During a stormy fortnight last winter when boats were unable to get through, Jimmy flew stores to us.

The press interviewed Jimmy who said:

> I can't leave my passengers on the island when they are due back in Perth ... they won't go for the weekend unless they're sure they'll get back by Monday.

Nearly 70 Rottnest residents signed a petition headed *WE WANT WOODS Get Him In The Air.*

The Regional Director of DCA in Western Australia, David Ross, who had always been sympathetic towards Jimmy, said he did not consider Captain Woods had acted dangerously when he flew an Anson from Rottnest into an easterly wind.

Jimmy sent a telegram to Air Minister Townley, asking him to intervene. He also wrote to Senator Agnes Robertson who spoke strongly in favour of his licence being reinstated, basing her support on the inconvenience to families planning school holidays on the island. And Jimmy himself flew to Canberra to make a personal plea. His determination and the massive public support paid off and he won a right of appeal.

The Board of Review met on 27 July 1956, combining the suspense of a major criminal investigation with the comic relief of a Gilbert and Sullivan operetta. It was held in the Institution of Engineers building and the Chairman was the Deputy Commonwealth Crown Solicitor, WJ Roberts. As the Crown Law Department acted for DCA, Roberts' appointment could hardly be seen as impartial. Nor could that of RC McGilvray, an employee of DCA. The other member, GS Griffen, an ANA pilot, appeared to be the only one of the three who was independent.

On his opening remarks, lawyer Francis Burt, acting for Jimmy, pointed out the misgivings he felt about the Board, especially:

> . . . as we are now faced with the position that the Client

[Director General of DCA] is appealing to a Board, the Chairman of which is his solicitor.

As the day went on, L R Edwards, appearing for the Department, used all the past evidence he could find to show that Jimmy had wilfully disobeyed safety regulations. His first witness was Captain Brady, the MMA pilot whose aircraft had flown back empty from Rottnest on 21 May.

In cross-examining, Burt established that the length of the controversial strip was adequate and that on that day in question Jimmy had appeared to clear the hills comfortably. As Burt continued questioning each witness, it became apparent that his defence was going to hinge upon the effective length of the runway and the obstacles which were allegedly involved.

When Carn Scarlett Wiggins, Assistant Director General of Operations for DCA, was questioned by Edwards, he referred to the real nature of the obstruction that had caused the Department to be overly cautious in deciding the effective length of the runway.

It was 'the dummy gun'. It had not been referred to before.

This dummy gun — built of wood and surrounded by camouflage material attached to four wooden posts — had been erected during World War Two, and was intended to mislead the enemy. It could be found at the eastern end of the runway on a small hill to the right of the army huts.

Francis Burt did not at that time pursue the dummy gun question, but concentrated on the way in which safety regulations were established.

'In regard to safety', replied Wiggins, 'I write the law'.

There was an uproar in the court, and when Burt asked whether he knew if the dummy gun was still in place, Wiggins admitted that he did not, but that it had been used in his calculations.

The next witness was David Ross, who under cross-examination conceded that there had been no restrictions imposed upon take-off from the cross-strip until 1955. Prior to that time the strip had been used in both directions with an average of 30 take-offs each week. Pressed about the number of accidents during those years, he conceded there had been none. He said that his only reason for wanting Captain Woods to give up flying into the wind was that 'regulations were regulations'. But he would not — could not —

171

say that what Jimmy had been doing was a highly dangerous operation.

Burt produced a map of the Rottnest strip and asked if Ross could calculate, from the regulation, the effective operational length at Rottnest.

'I thought I could', said Ross. 'I thought so until I referred it to Head Office and I found I couldn't.'

The reason for his confusion was that Head Office had not used the army hut on the hill at the eastern end of the runway as the obstacle that must be cleared, but another obstruction — the dummy gun.

When questioned further, Ross admitted rather quietly that as far as he knew there was no longer any dummy gun (except on paper in Melbourne).

'In fact', persisted Burt, 'it was eaten by white ants ages ago'.

'I understand it was made of pine', agreed Ross.

Nevertheless the four wooden posts which had held the camouflage material around the former 'gun' were still there, even though they fulfilled no useful purpose and could easily be pushed over.

The Enquiry Chairman then asked Ross:

> In your opinion, have the actions of Captain Woods in relation to flights between Maylands, Guildford and Rottnest been reasonably safe?

Ross replied, 'Yes, reasonably safe'.

It had been difficult for David Ross. He was one of the officers who had always maintained a staunch regard for Jimmy. But, as an officer of the Department, he had to uphold its policies. During the cross-examination he must have felt that in trying to be fair to both parties he came close to pleasing no one, least of all himself.

Burt continued to pursue the dummy gun issue. He called to the stand Warrant Officer Wilfred Sankey, who had been present when the gun was being built during the war. Sankey said:

> I went back in 1952 and all I could see was grass. The dummy gun had been weather-eaten and moth-eaten and everything else. The dummy gun is in fact, non-existent.

Then it was Jimmy's turn to be called. He had never noticed the dummy gun, he said, and the new regulation meant he would have to run his airline at a great loss.

Edwards, cross-examining, referred to Jimmy's various infringements. Jimmy, in his own defence, said he thought that the least DCA in Melbourne could have done when he sought clarification of the new regulation was 'to have had the decency to say, "We have allowed you to do this all these years, but now you must stop"'. There had been no such warning, he claimed.

The final witness was DCA officer Phil McCulloch who said that any timber likely to prove hazardous had been cleared away and burnt during the surveying and construction of the Rottnest airstrip, but that the four posts at the dummy gun site had not been removed because they had no relevance to the safety of the take-off.

'The critical object [the dummy gun] was located by our Head Office in Melbourne but we were not aware of it', he concluded.

With Burt stressing that DCA officials had said there was nothing unsafe in what Woods had done, and Edwards referring to Woods' past history of contravention and evasion, it was left to the Board to come to a decision. As they retired, speculation went on in the court room. Would Jimmy's appeal be upheld? Was it to be the end of Woods Airways?

At last the three men returned:

> The Board . . . has come to the unanimous conclusion that the Director-General's decision shall be varied . . . Having considered its obligations both to Captain Woods and the community at large, the variation will be such as to effect a suspension of Captain Woods Commercial Pilot's licence for a period of four months, operative from the date of the suspension which occurred on May 25th, 1956.

On the whole Jimmy felt that he had been vindicated. The *West Australian* ran a Leader article on 3 August, suggesting that it had been DCA rather than Woods that had been on trial. It urged that an independent inquiry be made into the operations of a department which could make and enforce a rule that deprived the public of a much needed service and a man of his livelihood.

Jimmy's friends and supporters, while relieved that his licence was suspended rather than cancelled, regarded the finding of the Review Board as disappointing. Jimmy, predictably, put the whole episode behind him, and filled in the time until he could get back into the air by sailing to Broome with Mollie and the Burts for a much needed holiday.

GROUNDED

There goes Woodsie!

Paul Rigby's seagull

Whether DCA decided to give Jimmy a break after the enquiry, or whether it was the other way around, there were few further additions to his Departmental file, except for routine entries relating to licence renewal and medical examinations. Newspaper coverage increased however, and Jimmy made front page news more than once in the *West Australian*, and was featured several times on the back page of the evening *Daily News*, by the cartoonist-columnist combination of Paul Rigby and Kirwan Ward.

In November 1958 there was a pilot's strike. Planes were grounded and passengers fumed at delays and the inconvenience of uncertain travel arrangements. All except passengers on Woods Airways.

'I own the airline', said Jimmy with slight overstatement, 'so why should I strike?'

Rigby's cartoon of 20 November showed a busy Jimmy wearing a variety of hats, dashing from office to airport, as baggage-handler and pilot, and Kirwan Ward wrote a piece attributed to a bemused tourist from Sydney who had encountered the one-man airline phenomenon.

175

Some time during the next few months, Jimmy upgraded the undercarriage arrangements. The next time Paul Rigby came aboard, Jimmy, as usual, beckoned him to the front seat and indicated the winder.

'I reached for it, started to crank and nothing happened. The old fox had electrified the winch and actually fell out of the cockpit laughing at my attempts while he casually pushed a button.'

Jimmy may have had cause to regret this electrification. On 5 August 1959, he was returning from a routine trip to Rottnest with a load of mail and fish, when the cut-off switch blew out the traction motor which lifted the wheels. An indicator showed the starboard wheel as down; the other wheel showed in the half-way position. Jimmy was not too concerned — he carried enough fuel for about 100 minutes flying time, certainly long enough for him to locate and rectify the trouble. He reported to Perth control tower and said he would let them know as soon as possible the precise nature of the problem.

He ripped the upholstery from the seat on the pilot's side to see if the chain reduction gear was working. It appeared to be in order. Then he tried to get at the other side to check the opposite wheel. The plywood on the seat was stubborn; it was impossible to remove it with his hands, and his tools were in the locker at the rear of the plane.

There was no automatic-pilot on the Anson so if Jimmy left the controls the plane would have to fly itself. He climbed to 3,000 feet, then put the aircraft into a gentle dive while edging back along the aisle to see how his weight would affect the trim of the aircraft. Then he dashed back to correct the plane's dive. By trial and error, first climbing then dropping, he got the Anson into the position he wanted. He made a dash to the rear, grabbed the tools and rushed back to the controls. With the plane once more on an even keel, he prised off the plywood panel only to find there was nothing he could do to rectify the problem. After contacting the control tower again and arranging for emergency landing, he flew around the City Beach area to burn up fuel.

At Perth airport, fire tenders, an ambulance and police waited. There was also a crowd of airport workers, passengers and others who had heard the news of Jimmy's plight. They watched as the Anson came in through rain squalls. It passed over the control

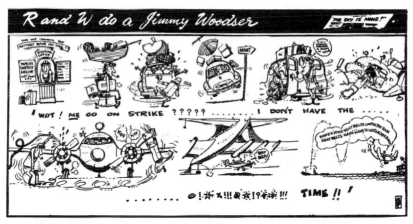

Daily News, *Thursday, November 20, 1958.*

tower but did not land. Jimmy did a second circuit of the field. Again he did not come in to land. Finally, on his third circuit, he brought the Anson in. It touched down its starboard landing wheel. Then the port wheel touched the ground and finally the tail dropped.

'Good on you Jimmy!'

There was spontaneous cheering from the crowd. Before the fire tenders had reached the plane, the motors stopped and the Anson slowed down. While it was still moving, Jimmy jumped out and ran alongside, pushing on the starboard wing to stop the aircraft rolling onto the grass. He said that he had not applied the brakes because that would have put an additional strain on the undercarriage.

The drama had lasted more than two hours yet Jimmy had emerged cool and apparently unperturbed. In the subsequent examination of the aircraft's equipment, it was found that some studs had snapped in the gearbox which lifted the wheel.

Although Jimmy had upgraded the Ansons with electrically operated landing gear, and had installed radios some years before, he still operated in much the same way as always, relying upon instinct and visibility. Rarely would he let the weather stop him taking-off. Sometimes on a winter's afternoon an air traffic controller might say,

'Jim, the weather at Rottnest — it's no good. It's closed in. You

177

can't get in there.'

Jimmy would look disbelieving and, barely shifting the stem of his pipe, would say,

'I'll just go and have a wee look'.

They couldn't stop him taking-off from Guildford if visibility there was all right, so he would take-off for Rottnest. According to Bob Pritchard he would always manage to find a way to get around the cloud — or under it. Then, if he did strike bad weather, he would open the storm window beside him and lean out to watch the ground directly below. It was what he had always done and he saw no reason to alter his methods.

Jimmy Woods — *Woodsie* — was a legendary figure by this time. His passengers were his friends, even if he had never met them before. He dressed like a gentleman farmer — tweed jacket in winter, short-sleeved shirt and drill shorts in summer, and a rather shapeless hat on his head. And of course, his pipe.

'He never really smoked the thing', said Bob Pritchard. 'But he'd smoke a whole box of matches, trying to light up.'

'Often the pipe would be upside down in his mouth', said Frank Colquhoun. 'The friction from the wind [in the early days of open planes] would burn its outer edge.'

In November 1960, DCA brought in a regulation that required all pilots over 60 years of age to have a second pilot — they could not fly alone in command of an aeroplane. For Jimmy to employ a pilot on full salary would have put impossible financial strain on Woods Airways. The regulations could not be withdrawn, or amended to suit his case. There was mounting concern in Perth that the regulation would, in effect, put Jimmy out of business.

Officials in DCA in Perth were also concerned. Of course there were those who saw a way of closing Jimmy down without any direct effort on their part — and they would avoid being accused of victimisation. But there were others who genuinely liked Jimmy and wanted to help him. The upshot was that two senior DCA men, Bob Pritchard and Bill Scott, agreed to fly with him provided his airline schedules could be altered to fit in with their off-duty hours. Jimmy was happy to oblige, and one of the men accompanied him on each flight. They did this in a voluntary capacity and in their own time.

Bob Pritchard always had a high regard for Jimmy:

He was a very hard working chap. He'd be there first thing in the morning and work on the aeroplane until he was due to go to Rottnest. Or he'd return from Rottnest, take the passengers into town, come back and service the aeroplane, then change out of his overalls and fly to Rottnest again. You couldn't help but like Jim. If you ever got mad at him, which wasn't hard to do, you couldn't stay that way for long. If Jimmy decided he was going to do something there was no way you'd change his mind. It was better to help him and make sure he did it safely.

Bill Scott, Jimmy's other co-pilot during this period, had a high regard for his flying skills:

'He could bring that aeroplane [the Anson] down as though it was a bird'.

Bill Scott also added to the stories of Jimmy's unorthodox behaviour:

One day I was with Jim on the way to Rottnest with a full load of passengers. I was piloting the plane. Jim suddenly looked at his watch and leaned over and closed off both throttles. I thought, 'Oh well, Old Jim must have decided to finish it all'. We were at about 6,000 feet so I put the plane into a glide mode. We were losing height pretty rapidly. After a couple of minutes (we were down to about 1,600 feet by this time), Jim looked at his watch again, leaned over and opened the throttles. 'Armistice Day', he said. 'Two minutes silence'.

The stories became legendary, yet, even as public affection for Jimmy increased, the odds against Woods Airways' survival also increased. It seemed to Bob Pritchard that it was only a matter of time:

The beginning of the end, as I saw it, was 5 November 1961. It was a Sunday morning (I was flying the aeroplane) and we had a full load of passengers, plus Jim had loaded all the Sunday Times in the back locker. You know, it was overloaded. Anyway, I took off and got to about 50 feet and there was a loud explosion in one of the engines — a major failure and [it] lost most of the power. The smoke was coming back through the duct in the wing to the cabin behind. I called the tower and said I was making an immediate landing on one of the cross runways. So I pulled the power and was starting to go back in there and Jim looked up and said, 'What are you doing?'. I said 'We're landing again, Jim'. I don't think he realised what had happened. At that stage we were battling . . . we were about 50 or 60 feet above the ground, belting around. We took it in and Jim chartered another aircraft from Millers to take the passengers over to Rottnest. He was very sad. 'It looks like the end of it', he said. But he had some spare engines and I said, 'Look Jim, I suppose we can get the motor out and change it'. He was all fired-up again. So we did that. We pulled that motor out on the Sunday and put another in and we flew it again on Monday.

But Jimmy had been right in his prediction. It was going to be 'the end of it'. The Ansons were getting old. They had been in service of one kind or another for almost 20 years; there was some concern about the glue that held the fabric in place. At the end of 1961 all Ansons were banned from flying over water or carrying passengers.

For a while Jimmy thought about negotiating to buy a larger aircraft but decided instead to call it a day.

Woodsie's last flight from Rottnest took place on 29 December 1961. More than 1000 people crowded onto the airstrip while the Premier of Western Australia, David Brand, paid tribute to 'one of the characters who have helped make Australia great'. Jimmy wore a garland of flowers and the crowd sang 'For He's a Jolly Good Fellow' as he and Mollie climbed aboard the Anson, waved to them all and took off for Perth.

As Jimmy flew over that stretch of water for the last time in a Woods Airways plane, Paul Rigby's seagulls waved and wept [see page 181].

Woods Airways was wound up, its shareholders paid out, and Jimmy arrange to dispose of the Ansons, obtaining a special licence to ferry them to their new owners. On 17 March he delivered VH-WAB to the property of some friends, the Gazes, at Gnowangerup, where Mollie watched as he flew in and landed. Jimmy wrote in his diary that night:

> . . . Mollie watched poor old faithful land in a paddock to be scrapped. But in a good home. It was a very sad day for Mollie and myself.

180

Last Rottnest flight. Jimmy Woods and Premier David Brand, 1961.

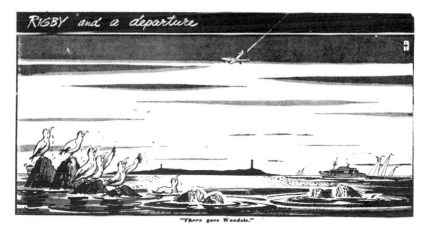

Daily News, *Friday, December 29, 1961.*

VH-WAB at Gaze's farm, Gnowangerup.

On 25 March, Jimmy flew VH-WAC to Peter Seabrook's farm at York and this time wrote, 'I was very sad to leave her'.

Jimmy put the past behind him without regret and got on with living for the day. Although he no longer had his Ansons, his Mosquito was still in a hangar at Guildford. When the possibility of selling it profitably had foundered, along with the original reason for its purchase, the aircraft which he had acquired with such high hopes became, perhaps without his knowing it, a symbol of the cherished dream of being a record-breaker: a race winner.

Jimmy had left the aircraft in the hangar for years, resisting requests from ANA to remove it until finally, in April 1959, needing the space, they demanded its removal. It was shifted to the DCA hangar where it stayed until 1960. Jimmy, in the meantime, had been negotiating with MMA to move his workshop/office, the two Avro Ansons and the Mosquito into the MMA building. When that space became available, Woods Airways operated from there until the company closed down.

Now Jimmy was to begin a new campaign:

WANTED: HOME FOR MOSQUITO
Veteran Pilot wants an aircraft museum erected at Perth airport to house his World War 2 Mosquito bomber.

So ran the newspaper headlines on 20 August 1962.

Jimmy wrote to Shane Paltridge, the Minister for Air, who agreed to let him have a portion of land at Perth airport for such a purpose, but there were no further developments and Jimmy and Mollie flew to England for an extended holiday.

For Jimmy it was also going to be in the nature of a business trip. At 70, he was about to embark on a new career; operating a helicopter service, and he wanted to find out as much as he could from various helicopter charter companies in England. With the lifting of the embargo on the export of iron ore and the opening up of the North West for oil exploration, Jimmy saw a future in helicopters.

In January 1963, while in England, he received a telegram from the Western Australian Division of the Air Force Association asking for permission to display the Mosquito beside its newly-acquired Lancaster Mark VII in a special enclosure at Perth airport.

Jimmy was delighted because the 'Quokka' had been left out in the open since Woods Airways had ceased operation, and was a target for vandals. He cabled permission immediately and the aircraft was moved to a grassed area behind the terminal building next to the Lancaster; a cyclone fence surrounded them both.

At the same time as these negotiations were going on, Mollie set off on a motoring holiday in Europe with her friend, Betty Graham. They had been gone only a few days when Jimmy received the news that he was to be awarded an MBE to be conferred by the Queen during her visit to Australia in March 1963. There was no time to organise for Mollie's return; in any case Jimmy didn't want to spoil her holiday, so he flew back alone, arriving in Perth a few days before the investiture. He was met by his old friend Eddie Nicholson who would be one of his special guests at the ceremony.

On 26 March Jimmy recorded in his diary:

> This has been a wonderful day for me... we were all taken to the [Government House] billiard room for briefing ... We

had to walk up to the dais and bow to the Queen. She pins the medal on your left breast. She asked how I liked flying. All our invited friends and others I spoke to outside were thrilled to see me get the decoration. If only my darling had been there... Eddie took most of us to lunch at the Adelphi... a wonderful day.

By December 1963, Jimmy's company, Woods Helicopters, was established. When his newly- acquired Bell helicopter arrived by ship, he sought space to house it in the DCA hangar at Guildford, but DCA ruled that only aircraft from regular companies could carry out maintenance work at Guildford. Jimmy was advised to base his helicopter at Jandakot.

Predictably, Jimmy did not take 'no' for an answer. He went higher than the Regional Director David Ross, and wrote to the Director General in Melbourne. That letter was referred back to Ross, but Jimmy did have the doubtful satisfaction of being told that he could erect the helicopter at Guildford, provided all maintenance was done at Jandakot. That didn't suit him at all. Nevertheless he set about erecting the aircraft and put the main packing case to good use - a purpose that did not go down at all well with the new Regional Director, WE Bowd, who informed Jimmy:

> It would appear that the main packing case used for transporting the helicopter has been turned into an office/work-shop . . . the only accommodation which can be made available to your company for a very limited period is for the helicopter itself.

Jimmy was required to remove all packing cases and material. When they were still there two months later he was threatened with legal action. A few days later, he wrote to DCA apologising for the delay, and explained that although he had advertised the packing case for sale several times, he had not been able to dispose of it. Now, he said, he would be giving it away immediately.

Although his original intention had been to set up a service for charter work, Jimmy envisaged all sorts of other possibilities and applied for a student helicopter pilot's licence. He underwent some instruction and possibly would have flown himself had he not become so involved in management. Mollie can remember the

Jimmy watching one of his helicopters land.

phone ringing at all hours of the night. London. New York. Helicopter pilots wanting work or looking for accommodation or bringing one problem or another for Jimmy to solve. It drove her mad, she said.

Jimmy tried various ways to set up his maintenance shop at Perth airport. One idea was to acquire property adjacent to the airport and build a workshop and hangar there. Another was to lease portion of the Ansett/ANA hangar, but this would need a variation in DCA policy. As had happened in the past, Jimmy would not give up until he had exhausted all avenues. Finally, he conceded defeat and the company operated out of Jandakot, engaging in aerial surveys, aerial spotting, agricultural work, advertising, carriage of passengers and cargo, as well as offering joy-rides.

In 1966 the problem of the Mosquito rose again.

The Air Force Association had been pressing Jimmy to contribute to maintenance costs (which he steadfastly refused to do, arguing that as the Association charged the public to view the machine, it should be prepared to pay maintenance costs). Jimmy was then asked if he was prepared to donate the machine to the Association in order to prevent its further deterioration. When he refused to consider such a request, the plane was moved out of the enclosure and left on one of the 'back blocks' at the airport with only a few trees for protection. Vandals forced the entry door off its hinges and damaged the inside of the cockpit. Instruments were stolen and the upper surfaces of the mainplane were damaged by people walking on them. The aircraft remained there, deteriorating, a constant source of frustration for Jimmy.

In 1976, a Perth man who specialised in vintage cars and aircraft, James Harwood, offered to buy the Mosquito; but when he had dismantled it for trucking to Sydney he found it so badly damaged that he put it back in storage. A subsequent potential sale to an American dealer also fell through because of the damage. Then another American, David Kubista of Tucson, Arizona, a former United States Navy pilot, heard about the plane through a New York acquaintance and decided to buy it. He planned to reassemble the plane, repairing the damage and re-equipping it with four cannons and six machine guns.

Having made these plans, Kubista left the Mosquito in storage with Bruce Kelman and Company, shipping and storage agents. Jimmy received a Christmas card from him, full of enthusiasm about the aircraft's future. Both Jimmy and Mollie believed him.

In fact, the Mosquito was still in store on the Melbourne waterfront and Kubista could not be traced. Eventually unpaid storage costs resulted in legal action against Kubista and 'The Quokka' was auctioned to cover the costs. After the Australian War Memorial made a successful bid for the aircraft, it was taken to the de Havilland facility at Bankstown for restoration to become part of Australia's aviation history, as well as a fitting metaphor for its former owner; a man whose dreams may not all have been realised, but one who seemed to survive all odds, managing always to deflect defeat, transforming it instead into a kind of victory.

AFTERWORD

Retirement, Jimmy and Mollie, 1973.

Jimmy and Owen Gaze at Albany, with the Buick.

Woods Helicopters continued until April 1971 when Jimmy resigned and ceased to be associated with the company. The former operations manager, JA Jones, took over as general manager and the company became Westcopters.

Jimmy and Mollie retired to Albany, staying in the Gaze's holiday home until December 1974, when they moved into a little cottage in Sussex Street, the first home they had ever owned. Jimmy worked in the garden, kept his latest Buick immaculate, and did all the repairs and maintenance around the house. One morning as he was tiling the wall behind the stove, a job he had been working on for several days, he collapsed and was taken to the Albany Regional Hospital. He died a few days later on 9 May 1975.

On 16 November 1987, the Rottnest Island airstrip facilities were named the Jimmy Woods Terminal. One of Jimmy's admirers, Frank Cocks, flew Mollie in a single-engined Cessna over the route she and Jimmy had taken so many times in the past and she was guest of honour at the official naming ceremony.

BIBLIOGRAPHY

Books

Bain, M.A. *Full Fathom Five*, Artlook Books, Perth. 1982.

Bennetts, D.C.T. *Pathfinder. Wartime Memoirs*, Muller, London. 1958.

Bertram, H. *Flight to Hell*, Hamish Hamilton, London. 1936.

Brearley, Sir Norman. *Australian Aviator*, Rigby, Adelaide. 1971.

Dixon, C. *Amy Johnson, Lone Girl Flyer*, Sampson Low, Marston & Co, London. 1929.

Driscoll, I.H. *Flightpath South Pacific*, Whitcombe & Tombs, Christchurch. 1972.

Dunn, F. *Speck in the Sky*, Airlines of Western Australia, Perth. 1984.

Gwynn-Jones, T. *Pioneer Aviator; The Remarkable Life of Lores Bonney*, University of Queensland Press, St Lucia. 1988.

Harvie, E.F. *George Bolt, Pioneer Aviator*, Reed, Wellington.

McCulloch, P. *Aviation in W.A. in 1938* (paper).

Metherell, A. *1942; Escape From the Rising Sun*, Cambridge. 1988.

Miller, H.C. *Early Birds*, Rigby (Seal Books). 1976.